"LEAD THEM TO CHRIST THE TEACHING-BRIDGE WAY!"

These study courses utilize the "Teaching Bridge" approach which leads the students from practical instruction regarding their everyday interests to correlated spiritual instruction geared to meet the particular spiritual needs of their age group. The following courses are available:

► **FOR TEENAGE BOYS...**

MAN IN DEMAND—Teacher's Book
MAN IN DEMAND—Student's Manual

► **FOR TEENAGE GIRLS...**

CHRISTIAN CHARM COURSE—Teacher's Book
CHRISTIAN CHARM—Student's Manual

These courses are ideally suited for use in Christian Day Schools, Youth Clubs, Family Night activities, Church Schools, Vacation Bible Schools, and Summer Bible Camps. They may be ordered from your local bookstore or:

HARVEST HOUSE PUBLISHERS
1075 Arrowsmith
Eugene, Oregon 97402
Phone: 1-800-547-8979

D0071486

From everyday interests to correlated spiritual instruction.

TEACHER'S BOOK
To be used with *MAN IN DEMAND Student's Training Manual*

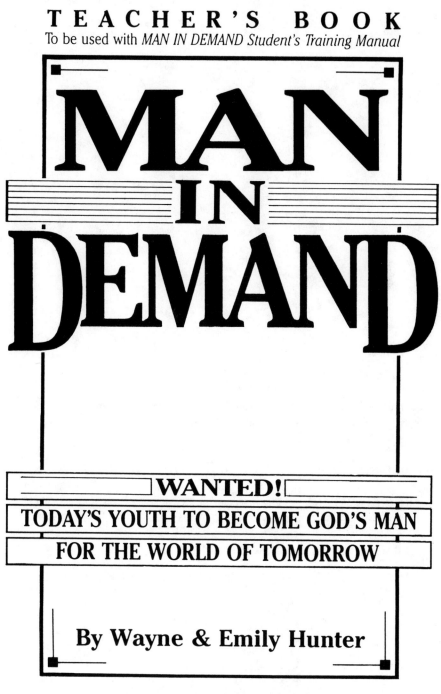

MAN IN DEMAND

WANTED!
TODAY'S YOUTH TO BECOME GOD'S MAN
FOR THE WORLD OF TOMORROW

By Wayne & Emily Hunter

HARVEST HOUSE PUBLISHERS
Eugene, Oregon 97402

MAN IN DEMAND TEACHER'S BOOK

Copyright © 1975 by Wayne J. Hunter and Emily Hunter
Published by Harvest House Publishers
Eugene, Oregon 97402

ISBN 0-89081-511-9

Printed in the United States of America.

CONTENTS

THE CHALLENGE OF A BOY
By Vivian Bruck

Is there any other challenge like the challenge of a boy,
With potential in his bosom to bring heartache
    or great joy?
Is there anyone sufficient to direct, to train, to guide,
And to bear the awesome honor of a tutor by his side?

For a boy is crammed with energy, with forces
    from within
That will mark the world with blessing
    or will curse the world with sin.
He is made by God in Heaven to assume the role of man
And to have dominion in this world — according
    to His plan.

Oft we see him in his childhood as just one of
    millions more,
With delightful, harmless interests and with
    weaknesses galore;
With remarkable, keen instinct to acquire the
    names of cars,
To aspire with wild ambitions, or deplete the cookie jars!

Oh, a boy can be demanding, and embarrass everyone,
So completely inconsiderate, pursuing only fun.
He can be so irritating, so neglectful, and so slow
'Till despair almost o'ertakes us that to manhood
    he will grow.

But a boy is often needy, filled with insecurity,
With a deep, unspoken hunger for our adult company;
He is looking for that training which we know
    he'll surely need
To fulfill a boy's assignment in a world of sin and greed.

An unspoken cry is written in the heart of every boy:
"Give me discipline, affection — not another plastic toy!
I am striving with the turmoil of the boy I'd like to be,
And the boy I have to live with — that's the boy
    who's really me."

He's confused and he is searching, he is hoping
　　there may be
Some true friend along life's pathway who will
　　understand, and see
Not the rough, exterior coating, but the tender
　　heart inside;
Not the evident reaction, but the reason he would hide —

Inner cravings, tears and heartaches, all the deep
　　unspoken fears
That have come from life's cruel battles; the resultant
　　marks he bears.
He is longing for a guardian who will listen to his tale,
For some real communication with an understanding male,

For some guide posts on his pathway, some direction
　　on his way,
That enable him to travel with a purpose in each day,
For the answers to life's questions, for release from
　　guilt of sin,
Restoration with his Maker, and a lasting peace within.

There just isn't any challenge like the challenge of a boy;
There's tremendous life investment if the time
　　we will employ
Just to share the truth of Scripture, and to see his will
　　give way
To the Potter's precious molding as a yielded
　　piece of clay.

To believe His precious promises, to see the devil flee
As the grace of God unfolding reaches his humanity.
Oh, the infinite potential, oh, the satisfying joy,
Of enabling God in Heaven to transform and use a boy!

WHAT ABOUT THE TEACHER?

WHO CAN TEACH THIS COURSE?

Anyone can — including women!

The most satisfactory teaching situation, of course, would be that of a man teacher. Nevertheless, if a man teacher is not available, a woman can teach this material by following the detailed steps given in the Teacher Book. In some class sessions, however, a woman might find it desirable to bring in outside male assistance. A team teaching effort by husband and wife would be excellent.

WHAT QUALIFICATIONS ARE NEEDED?

If you know Christ as Lord and Saviour and have a real desire to help boys become the men that God would have them to be — you possess the basic qualifications necessary to teach the "Man in Demand" course for teenage boys.

You may feel that you are unworthy to teach boys the high standards of Christian manhood set forth in this course. This is a natural reaction. Every sincere Christian is keenly aware of his faults and failures. None of us measures up to the standards God has given us in his Word. **Yet the goal remains — and it must be presented to each new generation!**

Realizing, however, that you are "meet for the master's use" not in your own merits but in the merits of the One who has called you and washed you in His blood to make you a brand new creature in Him — you can enter into your task of teaching boys these high and noble ideals with freedom and enthusiasm. God will honor your sincere efforts by pouring out His blessings upon the class, upon each boy, and upon you, the teacher!

IMPORTANT INFORMATION FOR THE TEACHER

1. HOW TO USE THE STUDENT'S TRAINING MANUAL

Each student must be provided with a copy of the Student's Training Manual. You, the teacher, will also require a copy for your lesson preparation.

Preferably, do not allow the students to take their Training Manuals home until after the first 5 or 6 class sessions. Instead, gather the manuals at the end of each session. This will prevent the students from "reading ahead " and will thus insure keen interest during class time. Beginning with the lesson, "Eating for Physical Fitness," however, your students will want to make use of their Bible reading charts and exercise charts, etc. at home.

2. HOW TO ADJUST YOUR TIME SCHEDULE

If your class period does not allow sufficient time to complete your teaching on a subject, plan to finish the subject at the beginning of the next class period. Adjust your time schedule with an occasional review of previous lesson material. If your time allotment is limited, you may require two or more training sessions for each subject. Some chapters may require more time than others. Do not rush through them, or your students will miss valuable teaching.

3. HOW TO USE THE "MEMORY QUESTIONS"

A "Memory Question" together with a scriptural response, is included at the end of each chapter of your Teacher's Book. Each "memory question" and "answer-verse" has been chosen specifically to reinforce the teaching contained in that chapter.

You may want to write these questions and answers on a wall chart, adding the new question and answer before each session. Cover each "answer-verse" with a flip-sheet (taped at the top only) to be turned up to reveal the scripture verse as needed. At each session review the previous verses by asking the "memory question" and letting your students respond with the correct answers. At the end of the course your class will be able to answer all 13 questions with an appropriate scriptural response — a worthwhile achievement!

4. WHY THE "TEACHING BRIDGE" APPROACH?

Our Lord was often able to proclaim spiritual truths to people by first talking to them about their everyday concerns. What are the everyday concerns of teen-age boys? **Their physical development . . . how they look . . . how to treat a girl . . . how to carry on a conversation . . . what their attitudes should be concerning sex, drinking, smoking, etc.** The Man in Demand training program makes use of a boy's typical preoccupation with his developing manhood as a teaching bridge or channel through which Christ may influence his life. Each lesson first captures the boy's attention by practical instruction regarding his everyday interests, then moves on to correlated spiritual instruction showing him that only Jesus Christ dwelling within can produce **true manliness!** The "teaching bridge" method will allow you to teach more effectively and with deeper impact upon the lives of your students.

INTRODUCING THE MAN IN DEMAND

(Pages 4 — 5, Student's Training Manual)

WELCOME, FELLOWS!

Welcome to the "Man in Demand" Training Program. And congratulations for taking steps today to become the man God can use tomorrow — a real man who realizes his masculine potential in Jesus Christ!

Already you're beginning to shape up into that man you'll someday become. But one of the most challenging facts about your formative teen years is this: You can still choose the kind of man you will be! **Now is the time to commence to become the man you want to be!**

(Write this on the chalkboard.)

Some of you may be thinking, "Why make such a big thing out of becoming a man? Any guy can grow into one. Just give him three meals a day and enough time, and he'll make it! The world's full of those who did!"

Yes, the world is full of "adult-male-human-beings," but not every male is a real man! True manliness is more than turning twenty-one or reaching the 6-foot mark on the wall. If manliness were measured by the tape alone, we've already been outdone by the giants that lived on earth before the flood. But God found them so inadequate as "men" that he had to destroy them.

GOD IS LOOKING FOR REAL MEN

Why is God interested in your masculinity? Because he's looking for men with disciplined minds, sturdy bodies and hardy spirits . . . men who are ready to stand up for him and do a vital work for him in this day. God's work, you see, is not for cowards or slouches. To answer God's challenge demands a real "he-man"!

When Jesus walked on this planet, he called co-workers who were vigorous and masculine — bold men, filled with the Holy Spirit, who could stand the scoffings of the crowd, men who dared to risk everything for him! And God is still looking for young men like this today.

No sissies, weaklings or shirkers need apply — "nor the timid or the fearful" (see Judges 7:3), but only those who are willing to submit to Jesus Christ as their captain, to bear his name proudly, and to link themselves with him to receive supernatural empowerment for the task. For it is "not by might, nor by power, but by my spirit, saith the LORD of hosts" (Zech. 4:6).

A PERFECT SPECIMEN OF MANHOOD

"But," you might ask, "what's God's idea of a real man?" The answer is simple. He's given us a perfect specimen to look at — Jesus Christ! The Bible says Jesus developed physically, mentally, spiritually and socially. (See Luke 2:52.) Some fellows miss out on this kind of total manliness, because instead of developing a well-balanced combination of strengths like Jesus did, they focus on just one aspect of their development— body building, for example. The result? They become incomplete, "lopsided" men!

THE DANGER OF BECOMING A "LOPSIDED MAN"

Maybe you're thinking, "What does it matter if I become an incomplete, lopsided man? Maybe I want to be just a 'muscle-man'! Can't I settle for that if I choose?"

Sure you can! But if you do, you'll also have to settle for a life that falls short of its total masculine potential. And — like "muscle-man Samson" — you may also have to settle for personal defeat. For the hardest struggles you'll face in life won't be to win the 50-yard dash, and the hardest battles you'll fight won't be fist-fights.

An epitaph from a soldier's gravestone tells the story. It reads:
"Here lies a soldier the world must applaud;
He fought many battles at home and abroad.
But the hottest engagement he ever was in
        Was the conquest of self
        In the battle with sin!"

SPIRITUAL BATTLES AHEAD

Before your teen years are over, you'll face moral struggles and spiritual battles that can overpower you if you face them unprepared. You'll be fighting against an enemy who is clever and knowing. He knows your strengths and he knows your weaknesses. Any weak area in your life he'll use to his advantage. But God doesn't leave you helpless. He offers to equip you **thoroughly** for the battle. His total training program involves **all of you** — your physical life, mental life, thought life, moral life, social life, sexual life and spiritual life.

FOLLOW GOD'S PRINCIPLES FOR MANLY LIVING

God's principles for living are practical and workable. You can apply them to every problem you might face. The goal of this training program is to make you aware of these life-principles and to teach you how to use them to achieve total manhood. Here's what you'll be learning:

1. You'll learn how to cooperate with **God's health laws** to build physical strength, to achieve stamina and vigor, to build strong muscles and a firm physique.

2. You'll learn how to follow **God's moral laws** to build moral strength, to cultivate a clean mind, to learn respect for your sexuality, and to conquer habits that would enslave you.

3. You'll learn how to follow **God's spiritual laws** to build spiritual strength, to experience deliverance from guilt, victory over fears, and power in time of temptation.

4. You'll learn how to follow **God's laws governing social relationships** to build social strengths. You'll learn how to conduct yourself in such a way that people will like you and

want to be with you. You'll learn how to carry on a conversation, how to be courteous and mannerly, how to treat a girl.

A NEW PERSONAL IMAGE

"But," you may ask, "how will these things help me become the kind of man that's in demand by the world and by God?" Here's how:

As you develop these various strengths — physical, moral, spiritual and social — your attitude toward yourself will change. Gradually you'll develop a new self-image. You'll feel more self-confident and more worthwhile. But you won't be the only person to see yourself in this new light! Others will also see you differently! As others sense your new self-respect and self-approval, they'll view you with greater respect and greater approval also!

NEW OPENINGS FOR YOU

You'll soon discover that people will want you in their groups and on their teams.

- Instead of being ignored, you'll be noticed.
- Instead of being bypassed, you'll be included.
- Instead of being avoided, you'll be sought after.
- People will listen to what you have to say.
- They'll place confidence in your opinions and in your judgment.
- They'll value your friendship.
- They'll choose you to hold important offices.
- They'll entrust you with positions of leadership.
- They'll grant you special privileges, special places of honor and responsibility.

To sum it up . . . you'll find that the new personal strengths you acquire through this training will create a new picture of yourself, not only in your own eyes but in the eyes of others as well. And as a result, new doors of opportunities for serving God and man will open for you. You'll come into a new quality of life. You'll be set free to become the man God originally created you to be. For God has placed you here on earth to fill a special need — now — in this generation!

EVERY GENERATION NEEDS REAL MEN

This generation — as none other — is crying out for men of integrity. People are demanding leaders they can trust — men of stature — not only in the political world but in the industrial, professional and scientific world as well. They're filtering out the slovenly slouches and the flabby, ineffective characters in favor of the disciplined, wide-awake young men who possess manly strengths and sterling qualities.

This is the kind of man God is seeking also to help heal the world's hurts and solve its problems. You see, the man the world needs and the man God needs are **one and the same!** There's no difference between them!

ONE GOAL AND ONE DIRECTION

This makes it easier for you, fellows. You don't have to choose between serving the world or serving God. You need only one goal in life — to be exactly what God wants you to be; and you need to walk in only one direction — God's direction! For in following this **one goal** and this **one direction,** you simultaneously fill both needs! **You become the "Man in Demand" both by God and by the world!**

Refer students to "Wanted! Today's Youth to Become God's Man of Tomorrow" (Page 4, Student's Training Manual) and "The Man in Demand" (Page 5, Student's Training Manual). Ask several students to read one or more stanzas of the poem, reserving the concluding stanza for you, the teacher, to read.

Please note: The challenge to become the "Man in Demand" is also expressed in lyrics and music. You will find the song entitled "Is It You?" on the inside back cover of the Student's Training Manual. If some of your students are talented musically, encourage them to practice this number on a piano, guitar or other instrument so that they may be prepared to accompany your class as they sing this song. You may want to use this as a musical number for a Father-Son Banquet or other type of completion program at the end of this course.

Memory Question No. 1: What well-balanced combination of strengths did Jesus develop as a growing boy?

Answer: "Jesus increased in wisdom and stature, and in favour with God and man" (Luke 2:52).

FINDING OUT WHO YOU ARE

(Pages 6 — 13, Student's Training Manual)

Refer students to page 6, Student's Training Manual. Read together the Enlistment Qualifications for the "Man in Demand" Training Program.

ESTABLISHING YOUR PERSONAL IDENTITY

What qualifications are necessary to become a trainee in the "Man in Demand" Training Program?

Basically, you must face up to the questions, "Who am I? Why am I here? Do I matter? And do I matter to God?" And doesn't this make sense? For unless you're willing to grapple with these important questions regarding your personal identity, there's no logical reason to concern yourself about what kind of man you'll become. Therefore, the first step in our training program is to settle — once and for all — the matter of your personal identity!

Some fellows never really come to grips with the mystery of that "secret person living within them." They never discover the real meaning of their own personal existence. Because of this, their lives are empty and unfulfilling. Like many of this generation, they cry out, "Who am I?"

Who am I?

There's a sea of empty faces
Floating in the world today.
Can you hear their hollow heart-beat?
Can you hear the words they say?
    "Who am I? Who am I? Who am I?"
Like a seething, surging tide,
Like a moaning, restless wave,
Going here . . . going there,
Never finding what they crave,
It's a seeking generation,
And it hollers with despair,
Shouting, "Tell me, is there **'something'** . . .
Is there **'someone'** way out there?

Shall we try to find nirvana?
Will we find true meaning there?
Shall we turn into a guru
Wearing long, flowing hair?
Does the zodiac know me?
Can I trust my lucky star?
If there's nothing more to living
Than this strife and clashing jar,
Why this hollow voice within me
Crying, **'Find out who you are!'**
Why this haunting song that whispers
As I strum my lone guitar,
    'Who am I? Who am I? Who am I?' "

Why haven't such persons been able to find out who they are? Because in seeking the answer to this question, they've looked in the wrong places. They've looked either to themselves, to others, or to the limited reasonings of limited men.

The next pages of our Training Manuals depict some of the pitfalls of fellows who follow this route.

JOE'S FUTILE SEARCH FOR IDENTITY
(Page 7, Student's Training Manual)

On page 7 we meet a fellow named Joe. Though Joe's search for identity leads him to a disastrous climax, it begins in a natural sort of way with Joe holding some quiet conversations with himself much as you or I might do.

Assign each of Joe's 6 conversations to a student to read aloud. You, the teacher, may provide continuity by reading the explanatory remarks at the beginning of each of the 6 stages in Joe's struggle for identity.

BEWILDERED BILL'S DILEMMA
(Page 8, Student's Training Manual)

While the search for identity leads some (like Joe) down dead-end roads, it leads others into a confusing maze. Take a look at Bewildered Bill on the next page. Why is he in such a dilemma? What kinds of thoughts are swirling about his head?
(Read aloud the 6 questions that are perplexing Bewildered Bill.)

If Bill actually believed these suppositions to be true, how would he feel about life in general? How would he feel toward himself? And toward others? How would you feel if you personally believed these suppositions to be true?

Encourage the students to express their views. Then read Bill's closing remarks in the two paragraphs at the bottom of the page.

GOD SAYS I AM "SOMEONE"!
(Page 9, Student's Training Manual.)

Bewildered Bill has now turned to the only satisfactory source of truth about himself. What does God say about guys like Bill or Joe . . . or you or me? God says we are each an important "someone"!

Write on the chalk board:

"Nobody's a 'nobody' with God!"

Whereas Satan would have you feel that your life has no purpose (and therefore it doesn't matter what you do with it), God says, "You're here for a reason!" Whereas Satan would have you believe that you're just another animal (and therefore you may as well live like an animal), God says, "You are **man,** and I've made you to have dominion over the animals! **I've crowned you with glory and honor!"**

Have your students read the verses from Psalm 8 at the top of page 9.

Note: These verses describe man's high place in God's order. The basis for this privileged place in creation is that man is made in God's image. This image, though marred by sin, has not been completely effaced. Man still bears the stamp of God's image upon him. (See 1 Cor. 11:7.)

Ask your students the following questions. Let them answer by reading from their Training Manuals as directed below:

How did we come into being?
(Student may read No. 1 from Training Manual.)

How do we happen to be here, alive on planet Earth?
(No. 2, Training Manual.)

How do we receive our continuing life-support on this planet?
(No. 3, Training Manual.)

Why were we created? What is the purpose of our existence?
(No. 4, Training Manual.)

What unique characteristic sets us apart from the animal creation?
(No. 5, Training Manual.)

What privilege does this give us?
(No. 6, Training Manual.)

What is the basis for man's dignity and worth?
(No. 7, Training Manual.)

GOD EVEN KNOWS MY NAME!
(Page 10, Student's Training Manual)

Allow time for students to read this entire page silently. Ask each student to write in the spaces allowed (1) his "given" name, (2) his "surname," and (3) his birth date and place.

Do you feel that someone really knows you if he doesn't know your name? Is it disconcerting to have a new teacher at school call you by someone else's name? Our names are special to us. We like for people to know them and use them. The name you've just written in your Training Manual is not only important to you, it's also important to God.

NAMES ARE GOD'S IDEA

It was God himself who first conceived the idea of attaching names to people. It was God who named the first man, Adam. It was God who changed Abram's name to Abraham, and Jacob's name to Israel. It was God who chose John the Baptist's name. It was God who chose the name for His Son, Jesus. And the angel whom God sent to earth to convey this fact also had a name — Gabriel! But the names of angels are not the only names in Heaven! The Bible tells us that our names are also recorded in Heaven! And we're told to rejoice because of this.

GOD'S KNOWLEDGE IS NOT LIMITED

God knows each of us by our individual names. Because our minds are limited, this fact seems hard to believe. In our limited human understanding, we're tempted to reason this way: "Billions of men have lived on earth since Adam. How could God possibly know each one by name?" But God is not limited as we are. The Bible tells us that God "telleth the numbers of the stars" and "calleth them all by their names." **All of the stars! And their number is as the sand upon the seashore!** If God calls all of the stars by their names, should it amaze us that he knows the name of every person who has lived on earth?

GOD KNEW YOU "BEFORE YOUR BIRTHDAY"!

If our names are important to us, no less important are our birthdays! We like to have people remember our birth anniversaries. And we like to talk with people who saw us on the day we were born. But according to the Bible, God saw us **even before we were born!** Listen to these words of David in a psalm of praise to God:

"For thou hast possessed my reins: thou hast covered me in my mother's womb. My substance was not hid from thee, when I was made in secret, and curiously wrought in the lowest parts of the earth. Thine eyes did see my substance, yet being unperfect; and in thy book all my members were written, which in continuance were fashioned, when as yet there was none of them" (Ps. 139:13, 15, 16).   Yes, God knows you **personally!** Rely upon it!   Think on it!   He knows your name.   He knew you when you were born. He knew you even before you were born. You're not just "another face in the crowd" to God! **You are personal to him!**

"I'M NOT JUST ANOTHER FACE IN THE CROWD!"
(Page 11, Student's Training Manual)

God knows you as a separate and distinct person. He knows the number of hairs on your head (Matt. 10:30). He knows the words you're going to say even before you open your mouth (Ps. 139:4). He knows the unexpressed thoughts that flit through your mind. He is the one person who is totally and thoroughly acquainted with you (Ps. 139:3)! Your words, your thoughts, your movements, your actions — everything about you is known to God — even your "sitting down" and your "getting up" (Psalm 139:2)! Yes, you are a special "someone" to God!

FINGERPRINT IDENTIFICATION
(Bottom of page 11, Student's Training Manual)

To help your students visualize the fact that God sees them as distinct individuals and has created them as such, have each student record his left thumb print in his own training manual, Space No. 1 at bottom of page 11. Provide a well-inked stamp-pad and a few paper towels. To obtain a clear print, have the student press his thumb into the stamp-pad several times, then transfer his thumbprint carefully onto the paper applying only moderate to light pressure. (Heavy pressure will cause the print to smudge and blur.)

After making sure each student has written his name in his Training Manual, have the students pass their manuals from one to another, and on to another, until the students can no longer guess who might be holding their manuals. Call "Time," making sure each student is holding a manual. Now have each student place his left thumbprint in the same direction in Space No. 2 on page 11 of the classmate's manual which he is holding. After recording his thumbprint, have the student enter his name in the space provided at the bottom of page 12 (in the classmate's manual) for later verification. Collect and return all manuals to owners.

Now, challenge each student to try to discover which classmate placed a thumbprint in his manual. Let the students circulate freely so as to compare the "known" thumbprints (in Space No. 1 of their classmates' manuals) with the "unknown" thumbprints (in Space No. 2 of their own manuals).

Note: If your class is large, divide into several groups for this activity as it would prove too time-consuming for each student to have to check out a large number of fingerprints.

After six or seven minutes, call "Time." The students may now check their "detective work" by looking at the names written at the bottom of page 12. Ask the students who correctly identified the thumbprint owner to raise their hands. Congratulate these "super-sleuths"! Exhort those who were thus identified by their fingerprints to let this remind them that God made them unlike any other person in the world! Exhort those who could not be so identified, or those who had problems identifying their classmates, to let this remind them that God being greater than man has no such difficulty! Each person is distinct and unique in his eyes!

I AM UNIQUE IN THIS WORLD
(Page 12, Student's Training Manual)

MY DECISION
(Page 13, Student's Training Manual)

Have your students read pages 12 and 13 silently and thoughtfully. Then make comments as follows:

An important question appears at the bottom of page 12. "What shall I do with this person I call 'me'?"

Is there a special job for you to do on earth? Has God created you for a special purpose? **Absolutely!** Somewhere in this world is an empty niche waiting to be filled by **you!** A "reserved" sign has been hanging there from all eternity and your name is engraved upon it! No other person in the world can fill this niche. **It belongs to you alone.** If another tries to fill your place, he'll find he's a misfit — like a key which lacks the exact shape to open the lock. But God has been shaping you from birth to fill this place in the world — exactly!

HOW HAS GOD BEEN SHAPING YOU?

Think back on your life for a moment. What has happened to you? Especially good things? Especially bad things? Have you had hurts or problems? Have you been granted special advantages or opportunities? God has been shaping you by every circumstance he's allowed to touch your life. He's been shaping you by the people he's brought into your path and by the problems he's allowed you to encounter, so that you might build the specific strengths you'll be needing for the task. God is shaping you day by day into a special tool to be used in serving him and in serving the world.

"But," you might say, "how can God make use of me? I can't do anything!" Neither can a wrench do anything by itself! In the hands of a Master Mechanic, however, a wrench can perform important feats! And so can the most unlikely fellow when he places himself in God's hands! This is your decision. You can choose to restrict your usefulness by living for self, or you can choose to live creatively with God, thus filling the purpose for which you were born.

Remember, fellows, God has created only one "you"! Because you are unique, you are important to God — and to the world!

Prayer:

Father, it's good to know that each of us is personal to you . . . that you know the details of our lives . . . that you even know our names. Such total knowledge staggers our minds! One so great as you deserves our best. Help us to develop our full potential, so that we may fill a place of service both to you and to man, through Jesus Christ, our Lord. Amen.

Memory Question No. 2: What formula did Jesus give us for finding real meaning in life?

Answer: "Whosoever will save his life shall lose it: and whosoever will lose his life for my sake shall find it" (Matt. 16:25).

ACQUIRING CONVERSATIONAL SKILLS

(Pages 14 — 20, Student's Training Manual)

YOU WILL NEED: Props for Conversational Skit — (two each) paper plates, napkins, and forks. Two chairs placed at front of the room.

BEFORE YOUR CLASS BEGINS: Select two students to take part in Conversational Skit. (See page 30.) Spend a few minutes explaining their parts to them.

YOU CAN BECOME A "MOUTH PIECE" FOR GOD

Does God care whether or not you become a good conversationalist?

Yes, he does! For two reasons: First, because he knows that the ability to converse freely will make you a happier person; and second, because he wants you to be his "mouth piece" as you mingle with others. Satan wants you to remain tongue-tied. He's placed a gag in your mouth, and he wants it to stay there. Why? Because in this way, he's shutting off a tremendous source of power that could be used for God.

Do you use your gift of speech for God?

SOME MAKE EXCUSES

Some boys say, "Well, I'm just not much of a talker!"

That's what Moses said. But God replied, "Moses, who made your mouth? If I made your mouth, I can also help you use it!"

Other boys say, "I'm too young to speak to people about God."

That's what Jeremiah said. But God replied, "Jeremiah, don't say you're too young! You shall go where I send you and speak what I tell you." Then God touched his mouth and said, "See! I've put my words in your mouth!"

GOD WILL HELP YOU

If you really want to make an impact on the world today for Jesus Christ, God will put words in your mouth, too. This doesn't mean he'll transform you into an eloquent orator, but it does mean he'll help you talk with people wherever you meet them, just as Jesus did.

ARE YOU A GOOD CONVERSATIONALIST?
(Page 14, Student's Training Manual)

What kind of conversationalist are you? Can you talk easily and freely with everyone, or do you "freeze up" around certain people? By answering the questions at the top of page 14 in your Training Manuals, you can discover just where you stand. Answer the questions honestly. No one else needs to see your answers.

Allow time for students to complete the quiz.

Now add your "yes" answers. What's your score? The fewer "yes" answers, the better conversationalist you are. Do you have 3 or more "yes" answers? Then you require some training in this area. Do you have 9 "yes" answers? Don't give up! You can still become a good conversationalist. Actually, it's easy to talk to others when you learn a few simple techniques. Here are seven rules of conversation guaranteed to help you.

RULE 1: WHEN YOU DON'T KNOW HOW TO BEGIN, LOOK FOR "COMMON GROUND"!

Let's say you suddenly find yourself among strangers. Introductions have been made. An awkward silence follows. You search for something to say. Where do you start? Why not start right where you are — on common ground!

"But," you say, "we've just met! We have nothing in common!"

Yes, you do! You have at least three things in common:

First, you are both "somewhere." You share a common environment you can remark about. For example: If you're in an elevator, why not say, "This sure beats the stairs, doesn't it!"

Second, you share a common atmosphere you can talk about. "Nice day, isn't it?" Or, "Wish it would stop raining!" Remarks about the weather have saved many an awkward silence.

And third, you are both in the same time zone. You can speak about the time of day. You can say, "Is it three o'clock yet?" Or, "Do you have the correct time?" (Even if you're wearing a watch, this is still appropriate, for your watch may be running slow! Who knows?)

Don't think you must wait until you have something profound to say. Make use of common topics such as these (the environment, the weather, the time) for conversation openers. But while you're discussing the weather (or whatever starter subject you choose), don't forget to use your eyes to search out further conversational clues — just in case you're together awhile!

For example, if the other person has an armload of books: "Been to the library?" Or if he has a towel rolled up under his arm: "Going swimming?"

In the week ahead, watch for opportunities to start conversations. Practice looking first for common ground, and secondly for additional conversational clues. You'll be amazed at your success. Let's do some practicing right now as we look at these 3 conversational problems given in our Training Manuals (pages 14 and 15).

Refer students to Conversation Problem No.1. Ask a student to read the problem aloud. You may read the portion titled "The Simple Solution." Give the students time to write down their answers to the questions. Follow this same procedure with Conversation Problems No. 2 and No. 3, on page 15, Student's Training Manual. Suggested answers to the conversation problems follow:

Conversation Problem No. 1 — What do they have in common? Their science class. What could he say to Jean? How do you like our science teacher? Do you think he gives hard tests?

Conversation Problem No. 2 — What do they have in common? The ball game. What could he say to the girls? Are you enjoying the game? Do you think our team will win?

Conversation Problem No. 3 — What clue could he discover while looking at Mary? The guitar case. What could he say to continue the conversation? Are you on your way to a music lesson? Who is your teacher? How long have you taken lessons?

Now you know the easy way to begin a conversation and to carry it along briefly. But how do you maintain a conversation for a longer period of time? Let's say you're seated by the same person all evening. Do you simply jabber on and on, telling everything about yourself? Some boys have tried this; but the longer they talk, the more bored their friends become! These boys need to learn the second rule of conversation.

RULE 2: DON'T TRY TO DO ALL THE TALKING!
(Page 16, Student's Training Manual)

Have your students consider the 2 cartoons, "In the 'Game of Catch' " and "In the 'Game of Conversation.' "

Conversation is a two-way game. It's like a game of catch. Doing all the talking is like hanging on to the ball. What happens to a game of catch when you hang on to the ball? It's obvious that hanging on to the ball ruins the game! But did you know the same thing happens to the "game of conversation" when you hang on to the "conversational ball"?

On this same page let's compare "Bill the Blabber-Mouth" and "Larry the Listener." *(Have two students read the parts aloud.)* Which fellow gets Betty's vote for being the most fun to talk to? Larry the Listener, of course! No one enjoys the guy who carries on a never-ending monologue. Voltaire rightly said, "The secret of being tiresome is in telling everything."

What truth does Mr. "Blabber-Mouth" need to learn? *Have your students complete the statement at the bottom of page 16.*

Answer: GOD GAVE US TWO <u>EARS</u> AND ONE <u>MOUTH</u> TO BE USED IN THAT PROPORTION.

Mr. "Blabber-Mouth" also needs to heed the apostle Paul's warning that we should not focus all our thoughts on ourselves, but should also think about others. "Look not every man on his own things, but every man also on the things of others" (Phil. 2:4). If "doing all the talking" is the wrong way to keep a conversation going, then what's the right way? Our third rule of conversation gives the answer.

RULE 3: KEEP THE CONVERSATION ALIVE BY TOSSING OUT QUESTIONS.
(Page 17, Student's Training Manual)

You can easily sustain a conversation for hours, if necessary! All you have to do is to keep the "conversational ball" in motion. Toss it back and forth . . . back and forth. But how do you toss the "ball"? It's easy. You ask a question!

The art of asking questions is one of the most valuable conversational techniques you can acquire. What makes it doubly important is this: When you ask a question, you not only keep the conversation alive, but the other person feels you're interested in him as well.

To see what a difference this technique can make, let's listen to a conversation between "Rick" and "Marie."

CONVERSATIONAL SKIT

Prior to class, select 2 boys to read the parts in this skit. One, of course, will play the part of "Marie." Choose a boy who will not feel embarrassed playing this role, but will perform well. Remove pages 215 and 216 from your Teacher's Book to provide parts for each player. Note: If you prefer not to present this material as a skit, simply read the conversation aloud.

As the skit opens, "Rick" and "Marie" are seated side by side before the class, holding paper plates and napkins in their laps. Using a fork, they go through the motions of eating as they speak.

SKIT, VERSION ONE

Rick: Hi, Marie! This strawberry shortcake sure tastes good, doesn't it! It's my favorite dessert.
Marie: It is?
Rick: Yeah . . . I never get tired of eating strawberries!
Marie: *(Without enthusiasm)*, Oh . . .
Rick: I've been picking strawberries all week, and I still like to eat 'em!
Marie: *(Bored)*, Well . . .
Rick: Yeah, and if I pick fast enough, I make pretty good money! I'm saving for a ten-speed bike!
Marie: Hmmm . . .
Rick: Yeah, and I'm gonna travel to the coast next year with Bill.
Marie: *(Looking aside as though trying to find a way of escape)*, Well . . .
Rick: Yeah! Bill's already bought his bike! It's really great!
Marie: Ho . . . hum . . . *(Yawns loudly, closes eyes, droops head as though to fall asleep.)*

End of Skit — Version One — *(Players remain seated.)*

Discuss skit with class, asking these questions:

Was this a successful conversation? Why not?
What impression did Marie receive of Rick?
How many times did Rick toss the "conversational ball" her direction?

SKIT, VERSION TWO

Rick: Hi, Marie! This strawberry shortcake sure tastes good, doesn't it! It's my favorite dessert. What's yours?
Marie: *(Brightly)*, Oh . . . I'd say it's the wild blackberry pie Mom bakes at our summer cabin!
Rick: Oh? Do you have a cabin? Where is it?
Marie: In the Blue Mountains! They're beautiful! Ever been there?
Rick: Sure! I go fishing there with my Dad. And when we're not fishing, we're hiking. What do you like to do in the mountains, Marie?
Marie: Oh, I like to swim. . . . and hike . . . and study the birds. Have you ever noticed how many blue jays there are?
Rick: Sure have! They're so noisy you can't miss 'em! And have you noticed the wild pigeons?
Marie: Yes! And the woodpeckers, too! You know, Rick . . . I've counted as many as 14 different species of birds near our cabin, but I don't know all their names.
Rick: Say, Marie . . . I've got a Bird Book! Maybe you'd like to take it with you next time you go! Can I bring it over sometime?
Marie: *(Brightly)*, Sure thing! That'll be great! Thanks a lot, Rick!

End of Skit — Version Two

Discuss skit with class, asking these questions:

Was this a more successful conversation? Why?
What did Marie think of Rick? Why?
How many times did Rick toss the "conversational ball" her direction?
   He asked her . . .
   1. What her favorite dessert was.
   2. Where her summer cabin was located.
   3. What she liked to do in the mountains.
   4. If she'd noticed the wild pigeons.
   5. If he could bring her his Bird Book.

By asking questions, Rick not only kept the "conversational ball" rolling, but also made Marie feel she was important to him.

But now . . . lest you start asking questions indiscriminately, a word of caution is in order: Simply "asking questions" is no fool-proof guarantee of success.

Our fourth rule of conversation must also be taken into account.

RULE 4: IF YOU DON'T WANT TO AROUSE RESENTMENT, ASK THE RIGHT KIND OF QUESTIONS!

Consider the questions shown in our Training Manuals (page 17). Can you tell which ones are acceptable and which ones might arouse resentment? If you believe the person would receive the question well, draw an upturned mouth on the face. If not, draw a down-turned mouth.

Correct and discuss your students' answers as follows:

Questions 1 and 2 could offend. Since they're phrased in a negative manner, they could infer that the other person is lacking or inferior in these areas.

Questions 3 and 4 (though similar to questions 1 and 2) are not offensive. Since they're phrased in a positive manner, they show friendly interest and a desire to know the other person better. This is always appreciated.

Questions 5 and 6 could offend. They invade the other person's privacy. No one welcomes snoopy questions.

Questions 7, 8 and 9 are not offensive. Everyone likes to be asked for information (as in question 7), or for an opinion (as in question 8), or for suggestions (as in question 9). Questions such as these make the other person feel valuable and important.

Question 10 implies criticism, and therefore it could offend.

Now, add your correct answers and see how you scored!

You can become an expert at pitching "conversational balls," however, and still fail the conversational game! How? By not really listening to the answers after you've asked the questions! This brings us to our fifth rule of conversation.

RULE 5: WHEN OTHERS ARE TALKING, BE A GOOD LISTENER!
(Page 18, Student's Training Manual)

Of course, you may hear the spoken words with your ears, but "listening" involves your eyes, your mind and your heart as well. Jesus spoke of men who had "ears that did not hear." They had "listening faults" that no hearing-aid could correct! Do you? Four "listening faults" are shown in our Training Manuals. Let's take a look at them.

Have your students supply the missing words in the statements beneath the four illustrations. Give correct answers and discuss each "listening fault" as follows:

(1) A good listener does not interrupt the speaker.

Why become so impatient that you "cut in" on the speaker? The Bible tells us to be "swift to hear and slow to speak" (Jas. 1:19). The speaker may be working up to an important point. Why not give him a chance to make it? It's absurd to be so busy planning your reply that you miss what's being said. When you listen attentively, your reply will come naturally and properly — at the right time (when the other guy is finished)!

(2) A good listener does not daydream while others are talking.

Do you play the game of "catch" with your arms folded? Of course not! You might miss the ball when it's thrown to you. But do you ever daydream when others are talking? If you do, you might miss the "conversational ball" when it's tossed your way! And worse yet, the speaker might be awaiting an answer to a question you didn't even hear! Keep awake! Play ball! Continue the game!

(3) A good listener keeps his eyes on the speaker.

When you look the speaker in the eye, you gain in two ways: First, you learn as much from his facial expressions as from his words (perhaps even more); and second, you find it easier to remain attentive. If you let your eyes wander, your mind is sure to follow!

(4) A good listener responds to the feelings of the speaker and shows it on his face.

The Bible says, "Rejoice with them that do rejoice, and weep with them that weep" (Rom. 12:15). Show the speaker you're responding to his words. Smile! Nod approval! Enter into laughter with him! Why wear a dead pan expression on your face and discourage the speaker?

RULE 6: DON'T FAIL TO COMMENT ON WHAT'S BEEN SAID.

In making comment, you may express agreement or disagreement (tactfully, of course), or volunteer something from your own experience. But do say something! When you fail to comment, the speaker concludes that you're so bored that you want to end the conversation. Feeling rejected, he'll soon leave you alone.

Our Training Manuals depict a girl staring with dismay at a "tongue-tied clam." Because of this fellow's silence, she's drawn some wrong conclusions. Write down her thoughts in the spaces provided.

Ask several students to share what they have written. Here are some suggested answers:

> *"I sure must've bored him!"*
> *"I just draw a blank!"*
> *"My thoughts left him dead."*
> *"I didn't even rate a reply!"*
> *"I guess he doesn't want to prolong our conversation."*
> *"I may as well walk away and look for someone who thinks I'm worth talking to!"*

THE "CONVERSATIONAL WHEEL"

We've now completed a 3-point system for conversational success. We've learned first, to keep the conversation alive by asking questions; **second,** to listen when the answers are given; and **third,** to show interest by making some kind of comment. Our Training Manuals depict this 3-point system as a "conversational wheel." (See bottom of page 18.) To make the wheel spin, simply follow the rotation plan as outlined:

(1) **Ask!**
(2) **Listen!**
(3) **Comment!**

Ask, listen, comment! Ask, listen, comment! Do this, and your conversation will roll along as long as you desire! But before you start talking remember that as a Christian you represent the Lord Jesus Christ. Therefore you'll want to consider one final rule of conversation.

RULE 7: FOLLOW THE SCRIPTURAL PRINCIPLES THAT APPLY TO ALL CONVERSATION
(Page 19, Student's Training Manual)

Have your students study the illustrations of the "5 guys no one appreciates." From the list of scriptures given, students may select the verse each fellow needs to remember, writing the references in the spaces provided. Correct and discuss answers as follows:

Guy No. 1 needs to remember Ecclesiastes 5:3.

"A fool's voice is known by the multitude of words." The guy who indulges in unbridled talking is liable to speak unwisely, uttering exaggerations, secrets, gossip, boastings, or words that will offend. David said, "I will keep my mouth with a bridle" (Ps. 39:1). This is a good idea for all of us! If we fail to "muzzle" our mouths, they may run away like wild, unbridled horses!

Guy No. 2 needs to remember Philippians 2:4.

"Look not every man on his own things, but every man also on the things of others." In other words, don't focus continually on yourself and your special interests. Consider the other person, too!

Before you talk at length about your chosen topic, ask yourself: Is this something the listener can grasp mentally? Is it reasonable for him to be interested in this subject? If the answers to these questions are "no," proceed with caution! You may lose your listener!

For example, let's imagine what has taken place in the situation shown here with Guy No. 2 and his friend (whom we'll call Mary). Possibly Mary asked Guy No. 2 a simple question such as "What did you do Saturday?" In answer she received an unwelcome barrage of words — plus a demonstration!

"What'd I do? I repaired the engine on my car! Let me show you! You see, this fuel pump quit working, so I had to remove the alternator to get to the fuel pump. And then I had to remove the fuel pump and replace the diaphragm . . .

. . . Maybe you don't know how a pump works, Mary, but it's sort of like this: A cam in the block presses on a diaphragm and forces the fuel through a ball valve into the carburetor, etc., etc., blah . . . blah . . . blab, blab!"

Mary was undoubtedly sorry she'd ever asked the question! A better solution would have been to skip the car repair details and talk about something Mary knows more about. For example:

"What'd I do? Well, after I finished repairing my car . . . I took Mom downtown to a rummage sale. Mary, you should have seen the junk they were selling! Scratchy old phonograph records, 'n fur coats, 'n antique rockers, 'n old dolls! Do you like to go to rummage sales, Mary?"

Remember: People enjoy best the topics they know most about!

Guy No. 3 needs to remember Ephesians 4:29.

"Let no corrupt communication proceed out of your mouth." What is "corrupt communication?" Speech that is tainted, foul, or defiling — such as gutter language and swear words.

Actually, gutter language and swear words don't impress anyone! Everyone knows that the guy who cusses the most has **the least confidence in himself!** Take the apostle Peter, for example. When he sat by the fire the night Jesus was betrayed, he was too weak to admit he even knew Jesus! When he saw that his words were falling flat, he tried to beef them up with cursing. This is normally the case: **The weaker the man, the stronger his language!**

But what's wrong with using 4-letter words? The same thing that's wrong with looking at obscene pictures. Filthy words bring filthy pictures into your mind. And when you speak these words around others, you bring filthy pictures into their minds also. The Bible tells us to speak words that are "good to the use of edifying" (Eph. 4:29). This means words that are wholesome and healthful — words that build others up, rather than tear them down.

In Ephesians 5:4 we're told that our speech should contain no "filthiness, nor foolish talking, nor jesting." Does this mean we can't enjoy good, clean humor? No! Everyone enjoys a good laugh! What is forbidden are coarse, filthy jokes. But what can you do when the guys start swapping dirty stories? You can clean up the polluted atmosphere by telling some clean stories! Keep several in mind for such times. And learn to tell them well. Or simply ignore the dirty jokes and lead off on another subject.

Guy No. 4 needs to remember Proberbs 27:2.

"Let another man praise thee, and not thine own mouth; a stranger, and not thine own lips." In other words, **don't brag about yourself!** If you want others to feel good around you,

don't try to always appear great!   Instead, tell about the
times you've goofed! It's almost impossible to defame
yourself by telling about your foolish mistakes.

Why does a fellow boast? He's seeking applause from others.
But Pascal said, "If you wish men to speak well of you, then
never speak well of yourself." Applause comes from the
audience — not the performers!

Guy No. 5 needs to remember 1 Peter 3:8.

"Having compassion one of another, love as brethren, be
pitiful, be courteous." Don't exclude a third party from your
conversation. No one likes to be left out. Practice love by
showing compassion for others.

"LET'S TAKE A LOOK AT YOUR TONGUE, SON!"
(Page 20, Student's Training Manual)

Our Training Manuals suggest we give ourselves a "tongue
examination." Why does the doctor check our tongues?
Because they often indicate our general health. Our "tongues"
also reveal our spiritual health. For the Bible says, "Those
things which proceed out of the mouth come forth from the
heart" (Matt. 15:18). Let's compare the two columns of
scriptures in our Training Manuals to see which one best
describes the condition of our tongues.

*Let your students take consecutive turns, each reading aloud one
scripture verse until all scriptures have been read. Suggest that the
students take a silent check on their tongues as they listen to the verses.*

USE YOUR TONGUE FOR JESUS!

At the bottom of this page is an important question: What is
the best way to use your tongue, and what is the power that
will help you do it?

Ask a student to read Mark 5:19.

"Go home to thy friends, and tell them how great things the
Lord hath done for thee, and hath had compassion on thee."

The best way to use your tongue is to speak out for Jesus! He's one person you can brag about! After healing the demon-possessed man, Jesus told him to tell his friends about it. Has the Lord done something wonderful for you? Then tell your friends about it! Tell them he can do the same for them. Tell your friends that Jesus is a liberator who can set them free . . . that Jesus died on the cross to change the world's bad news to good news!

GOOD NEWS FOR ALL

What is the good news? Jesus says, "Come to me! Believe in me! I'll give you new life! I'll take care of your guilt problem! I'll forgive your sins! I'll release you from your fears! I'll help you live victoriously!" **That's good news — and it's for everyone!**

But you may ask, "How do I tell people these things? Do I stand on the street corner and shout them out, hoping they'll listen?"

FOLLOW JESUS' EXAMPLE

To be sure, God has made use of street evangelists, and many have believed on Jesus through their witness, but God has not called everyone to this ministry. Everyone, however, can follow Jesus' example. Jesus caught people's attention by talking about things that interested them — such as building houses and barns, planting crops, harvesting, or going fishing. But he didn't stop there — he used these common, everyday topics as "starters" to lead people into conversations about God.

You can do the same thing! You have learned how to open conversations and how to keep them rolling. Using these techniques, you can become a voice for God. The more freely and easily you can converse with others, the more opportunities you'll have to do this!

But some of you may be thinking, "Even so, I'm still afraid to speak out for Jesus!" If this is your problem, there's help available.

POWER FOR WITNESSING

Ask a student to read Acts 1:8.

"But ye shall receive power, after that the Holy Ghost is come upon you: and ye shall be witnesses unto me."

Peter at one time was too timid to say a single word in defense of his Lord. But that was before the Holy Spirit came upon him. **After Pentecost Peter couldn't keep quiet!** When the rulers tried to shut him up, he said, "We cannot but speak the things which we have seen and heard."

The same Holy Spirit can free your tongue and give you boldness. He can make Jesus' love so real to you that you'll want to share it with everyone! Ask the Holy Spirit to fill you with His power. **Then go — in that power — and be a "voice" for God!**

Two thousand years ago John the Baptist came as a "voice" proclaiming the first appearance of Jesus Christ. Today God is raising up many young voices to proclaim his second coming — to give out the message, **"Jesus is coming again!"**

Prayer:

God, help us to make skillful, careful use of your gift of speech. Keep us from "freezing up" around others whom you place in our path, and who may need the friendship of a fellow who believes in you. May we learn to talk freely with everyone — as Jesus did.

But God, keep us from becoming empty-headed blabber-mouths, interrupting others and selfishly monopolizing conversations. And God, may we not use our tongues to boast about ourselves — but to boast about You, telling others how great You are, and what a wonderful gift You gave the world in your Son, Jesus Christ! Amen.

Memory Question No. 3:

If we really want to use our gift of speech for God's glory, what should be our prayer?

Answer: "Let the words of my mouth, and the meditation of my heart, be acceptable in thy sight, O LORD, my strength, and my redeemer" (Ps. 19:14).

42

ACHIEVING A MANLY POSTURE

(Pages 21 — 28, Student's Training Manual)

YOU WILL NEED: Full-length mirror, string, adhesive tape and weight (to make plumb line mirror).

BEFORE YOUR CLASS BEGINS: Prepare plumb line mirror by taping a long piece of string at center top of mirror. Affix weight to the string slightly above the floor.

DOES POSTURE REALLY MATTER?

Maynard doesn't like to hear about his posture!

"Why should I try to straighten up all the time?" he complains. "If I'm a slouch, I'm a slouch! Why should I attempt to look like something I'm not — just to satisfy others?"

Let's take a look into Maynard's problem. Does it really matter how he stands or walks or sits, or is this just another convenient subject for his parents to "sound off" about? Our Training Manuals list 7 things every boy needs to know about the power of his posture.

Teacher: Follow the same procedure throughout each of the following 7 points regarding the power of a boy's posture. First, read and discuss the positive effects of good posture; second, consider together with your class the cartoons which show how a boy's posture can affect his life either favorably or adversely. Third, call your students' attention to the question beneath the cartoons. Have your students write down their answers. Allow them to share them briefly with the class. Suggested answers to each question are provided for you.

1. YOUR POSTURE CAN HELP YOU GET THE JOB YOU WANT!
(Page 21, Student's Training Manual)

Read and discuss the positive effects of a disciplined posture upon a boy's ability to secure a job. Consider cartoons. Have students answer question. Suggested answers:

A slovenly, indolent posture . . .
Invites distrust.
Discredits your physical abilities as a workman.

Weakens your own self-esteem.
Makes you appear to lack energy.
Makes you look lazy and tired.
Gives you an air of failure.

2. YOUR POSTURE CAN INCREASE YOUR MASCULINE APPEAL.

Read and discuss how a pleasing, straight posture affects a boy's masculine appeal. Consider cartoons. Have students answer question. Suggested answers:

A slouchy posture . . .

Makes you look like a "washout."
Gives an appearance of weakness.
Decreases your height.
Detracts from your manly appearance.
Makes you appear inferior and embarrased.
"Turns off" that girl you'd like to impress!

Please note: You may notice similar positive and negative effects reappearing in the 7 different points. This reemphasis is desirable, for similar effects can bring varying results according to the varying life-situations. For example: A posture which gives a boy an "appearance of weakness" will affect not only his masculine appeal (as in No. 2) but also his ability to get a job (as in No. 1) where this "appearance of weakness" may strike the prospective employer as a lack of energy or possibly even laziness.

3. YOUR POSTURE CAN HELP YOU PASS THE TEST AND MAKE THE GRADE!
(Page 22, Student's Training Manual)

Read and discuss how an alert posture affects scholastic performance. Consider cartoons. Have students answer question. Suggested answers:

A lazy posture . . .

Tends to reduce blood circulation to the brain, thus inhibiting its functions.
Contributes toward slower reactions and response.
Promotes dull, fuzzy thinking.

4. YOUR POSTURE CAN HELP YOU GET THE VOTES YOU NEED TO WIN!

Read and discuss how a strong, manly posture can help a candidate for office. Consider cartoons. Have students answer question. Suggested answers:

A weak posture . . .

Weakens your own self-esteem and thus the force of your personality.

Impairs speaking ability by inhibiting proper breathing.

Fosters disrespect and distrust from others.

Invites failure.

5. YOUR POSTURE CAN KEEP YOU FROM GETTING DEPRESSED.
(Page 23, Student's Training Manual)

Read and discuss how a resolute, soldierly posture can improve a boy's mental outlook. Consider cartoons. Have students answer question. Suggested answers:

A dejected, "whipped" posture . . .

Encourages mental depression.

Breeds pessimism.

Helps you succumb to your fears.

Hastens a hopeless surrender to problems.

6. YOUR POSTURE CAN INCREASE YOUR ENERGY AND VIGOR!

Read and discuss how a full-chested posture can increase physical vigor and performance. Consider cartoons. Have students answer question. Suggested answers:

A stooped posture . . .

Promotes physical weakness.

Undermines vigor and health.

Restricts lung capacity.

Saps body energy, thus inhibiting work capacity.

7. YOUR POSTURE CAN MAKE YOUR WITNESS FOR JESUS MORE EFFECTIVE.
(Page 24, Student's Training Manual)

Read and discuss how a strong, manly posture aids your Christian witness. Consider cartoons. Have students answer question. Suggested answers:

A spiritless, apologetic posture . . .

Dishonors your body as God's creation.

Repels the listeners and observers.

Is inconsistent with your words and therefore weakens their "punch."
Destroys the total impact of your witness.

GOOD POSTURE REQUIRES DISCIPLINE

Naturally you will want to exercise your "posture-power" in a positive way. You will want it to produce desirable effects within yourself and upon others. You will want your posture to bring credit to the one you represent. "But," you may say, "how can all this be accomplished?" **There's only one way — through discipline!** Discipline that trains and controls not only your muscles but also your mental outlook! For just as your posture influences your mental outlook, so does your mental outlook influence your posture!

BODY, MIND AND SPIRIT AFFECT YOUR POSTURE

Have you ever watched a derelict walk the streets of Skid Row with his drooping shoulders and shuffling gait? He has broken both the laws of health and the laws of God. He has damaged his body as well as his mind and spirit. He is a failure, without hope or purpose; and he shows it by the way he carries himself!

You see, a man's posture mirrors the condition of his mind and spirit as well as his muscles. When you think you are a failure, you droop your shoulders. When you feel bored and aimless, you drag your feet. When you feel guilty, you hang your head. On the other hand, when you think "success," you quicken your gait! When you think "confidence and courage," you lift your chest and hold your head high. And when you are filled with joy, every muscle seems to come alive.

YOUR MIND CALLS THE SIGNALS AND YOUR MUSCLES OBEY

Of course, it requires no physical effort for muscles to obey "down-beat signals" like "slump . . . sag . . . or droop," just as it requires no effort for an animal to simply give up and die! But to continuously obey "up-beat life-signals" requires well-conditioned muscles. Therefore it behooves you to keep **both** your mind and your muscles in good shape!

First, let your mind be made strong and confident through Jesus Christ. Then develop the muscle-power necessary to respond to the strong positive signals this kind of mental outlook produces. The result? You'll automatically stand straight as an arrow! You'll step out like a real man, full of confidence and vigor!

But your muscle training must begin **now!** Just as it's impossible to reshape concrete once it has hardened, so it will be impossible to reshape your posture when you are old. **Now** is the time to check up on your posture habits and to train your muscles to form good ones! **Let's get started right now!**

HOW TO HAVE A MANLY-LOOKING POSTURE
(Page 25, Student's Training Manual)

Have your students practice the various posture techniques throughout your instruction period. Make suggestions and corrections. As the various posture techniques are discussed, choose two students from your class to demonstrate. Let one student show the strong, manly way to walk, stand, sit, etc. while the other portrays the weak, slouchy way. By observing the contrasting movements and positions simultaneously, the students will recognize their own faults more readily. They will also become more aware of the detrimental effects of poor posture and carriage.

KEEP YOUR HEAD HIGH!

Let's attack the problem "head first!" For how you carry your head determines to a large degree your total manly appearance. A sagging head triggers a downward chain reaction that ends with a weak, slumpy appearance. **Try it** and see! Let your head sag. What happens?

1. Your shoulders slump.
2. Your chest caves in.
3. Your waistline thickens.
4. Your chest disappears into your stomach.
5. You've lost about one inch in body height.
6. You've added about one inch around your middle.
7. You've sagged all over like a dish of warm jello.

Frankly, you don't look good!   For good body balance and a trim appearance, keep your head high! Pull it up! No, not with your chin . . . pull from behind! Get the "feel" of it by pulling upward on your hair at the crown of your head. Stretch the top of your head upward until you feel a tugging behind your ears. At the same time let your shoulders drop downward. Keep as much distance as possible between your shoulders and your head.

KEEP YOUR HEAD CENTERED OVER YOUR SHOULDERS!

Never hang your head forward over your chest. Deliberately push back with your neck muscles until the center of your ear lines up vertically with the center of your shoulder bone. Ask the one next to you to check your head position by holding a ruler or pencil vertically at your ear lobe. *(Allow time for students to take this "Pencil Test" as shown in their Training Manuals.)*

Does the center of your ear lobe line up with the center of your shoulder bone? Push your head backward until it does! Keep your chin in, and the back of your neck against your collar.

KEEP YOUR SHOULDERS STRAIGHT, YOUR CHEST HIGH BUT RELAXED.

* Don't hunch your shoulders forward over your chest in a hawk-like manner; don't thrust them backward.

* Don't hold your shoulders high and strained. Exert a slight downward pressure on your shoulders to keep them low and relaxed.

* Don't puff out your chest unnecessarily. Puffing out your chest will thrust your shoulders backward in an awkward position and will produce a swayed back and bulging buttocks.

* Hold your chest high but relaxed. Hold it high enough to leave plenty of space between your hip bone and your ribs.

MAKE THIS TEST FOR YOURSELF!

(Have your students follow these instructions as you give them.)

Curve your shoulders into an exaggerated forward slump, caving in your chest. Now, maintain that posture and try to breathe normally.

(Have them keep it up for several minutes.)

Are you beginning to feel "oxygen hunger?" Do you need to take a deep breath? How well would you do on the 600-yard run?

Now, keeping your shoulders hunched over and without straightening up, try to take that deep, full breath you are craving. Inhale as much as you can! What happened? Did you expand your lungs like a fully blown-up balloon? Did the inflow of air push out every wrinkle and cavity in your lung sacs? **No, it was not possible in that position!** At best, your air intake allowed only a partial blow-up!

Although this is an exaggerated test-case, it illustrates how posture affects physical well-being. Although your shoulder slump may not be so pronounced as to produce **a greatly restricted** intake of air, even a slight shoulder hunch will produce **a slight restriction!** Why settle for second best? Give your lungs and yourself nothing but the best!

STAND STRAIGHT AND TALL . . .

Help your students assume proper posture as follows:

- Head pulled high and set squarely over shoulders!
- Chest high but relaxed!
- Spinal column straight . . . not hollowed! (A swayed back can cause serious back troubles when lifting, as it can overstress the spinal column discs thereby causing them to rupture.)
- Abdomen up and in, buttocks down and under. These two work together. As you tighten your buttocks muscles (pushing downward and tucking under), flatten your stomach at the same time (pulling upward and inward). This is a critical area. These muscles must be kept under control.

- Arms falling naturally at sides.
- Knees relaxed — not stiffly locked. Knees should be slightly flexed. If you lock them stiffly and tightly, you will protrude fore and aft in a figure "S" curve. Try locking your knees and see what happens! Do you feel your weight thrown forward and your stomach pushing out? Notice that your back is swayed and your buttocks stick out far behind.

INSPECTION TIME!

Check your students' postures by the plumb line test. Direct each boy to stand sideways in front of the mirror so that the plumb line is centered on the lobe of the ear. If his posture is in correct balance, the plumb line will bisect the body at the lobe of the ear, at the center of the shoulder bone and hips, and will come less than an inch in front of the ankle bone. The plumb line doesn't lie! If the body is off balance, help the student to realign himself correctly.

STEP OUT LIKE A MAN
(Page 26, Student's Training Manual)

You've learned how to stand. Now learn how to walk like a man! This is how you do it:

First, check your posture. Stretch up high. Assume good head and shoulder posture. Now, walk in a straight line. Imagine you're following a chalk line. Point your feet straight ahead. Don't toe in and don't toe out.

Remain vertical from the hips up. Are your head and chest slanting forward, trying to get ahead of the rest of you? Are you leading with your head and "pointing with your nose" like a Beagle hound? Get your head back in line over your hips. Keep your body vertical.

Don't bounce along! Allow some natural elasticity in your step, but don't jerk up and down unnecessarily. Of course your body will elevate when it is centered directly over the ankle. This is natural. It produces a rhythmic "rise and fall" which looks normal and manly. Extreme up and down motion, rather than looking manly and self-assured, appears juvenile, self-conscious and "put on."

AND WHEN YOU ARE SEATED . . .

FOUR SURE WAYS TO MAKE A BAD IMPRESSION

1. Recline in your chair, sliding your hips forward. This position carries a "double-whammy"! You'll look bad when seated, and you'll look bad when you're on your feet again; for you're almost sure to have hunched shoulders when you stand up!

2.   Become a "human pretzel"! Twist your feet around the legs of the chair! Intertwine your arms through the back supports at the same time! This is guaranteed to ruin your masculine appearance, for who can look like **a man   in command of himself**   when he's tied up in knots? If someone were to scream "fire," you would fall on your face (along with your chair)!

3. Sprawl like a "floppy dog." Curl up or spread out according to your whim! Let yourself go! With loose muscles and no restraint, it's easy to achieve the floppy dog look!

4. Assume the "cramped toe" position. With knees pressed tightly together, legs fanned out and toes turned in, you're sure to have a constricted, pinched appearance that will make you look less than a man!

THREE SURE WAYS TO HARASS YOUR HOSTESS

1. Tilt backward on her chairs! Don't be concerned about the strain you're placing on them! They may break under the strain, but why worry? They're not your chairs! To especially annoy your hostess, choose a fine old antique!

2. Stick your legs out into the room, so she can't possibly get by to serve refreshments! And if you really want to produce frustration, ignore her when she stands there helplessly with a heavy tray in her hands!

3. Don't use your leg muscles — just drop "kerplunk!" into her upholstered chairs. You never know . . . this might be the time the springs pop!

These actions, of course, are all examples of unkindness and discourtesy. This is **not the way to put** love in action. And this is **not the way to make** a favorable impression! (You'll get attention all right — but not the right kind!)

A SURE-FIRE FORMULA FOR COMMANDING THE RIGHT KIND OF ATTENTION

If you want to let the world know that you're a real man — here's the way to do it:

- **Sit tall!** Keep your head on your shoulders.
- **Sit erect!** Keep your thighs at right angles to your body with your legs under control.
- **Sit confidently** . . . relaxed and at ease!

This is the way to command respect, for you'll give the appearance of someone who's "sitting on top of the world" instead of one who is "crushed beneath it!"

DOES IT MAKE ANY DIFFERENCE WHERE YOU WALK . . . STAND . . . SIT?
(Page 27, Student's Training Manual)

DOES IT MATTER TO GOD?

Students may read Prov. 4:14, 15 and fill in blanks as instructed in their Training Manuals.

DID IT MATTER TO THE YOUNG MAN IN PROVERBS 7?
Have your students read Proverbs 7:6-27 and list 3 ways in which this young man was "stupid" (or void of understanding). Suggested answers:

1. This young man was stupid because he didn't heed the warnings in God's Word, but instead allowed himself to be tempted by a bold girl with a brazen face (v.13). He should have known her type for her dress revealed it (v.10).

2. This young man was stupid because he let himself become an easy dupe to her charms! First she flattered him (v.21) — and he fell for that. Then she caught him and kissed him (v.13) — and he fell for that, too!

3. This young man was stupid because he didn't stay clear of her path in the first place! He knew where she did her street-walking but foolishly walked headlong into the path of temptation. Proverbs 7:8 describes him as "passing through the street near her corner." **Couldn't he have crossed the street?** Instead, we read he "went the way to her house" (v.8).

4. This young man was stupid because he refused to look beyond that which was immediately in front of his nose, and thus became an easy prey to her well-set trap! We read that he "goeth after her straightway, as an ox goeth to the slaughter . . . as a bird hasteth to the snare, and knoweth not that it is for his life" (v.22, 23).

5. This young man was stupid because he thought he was so strong that he didn't need to avoid temptation! The closing words of this 7th chapter of Proverbs tell the fate of many so-called "strong men" who relied upon their own unguarded strength. "Hearken unto me now therefore, O ye children, and attend to the words of my mouth. Let not thine heart decline to her ways, go not astray in her paths. For she hath cast down many wounded: yea, many strong men have been slain by her. Her house is the way to hell, going down to the chamber of death" (v. 24-27).

In other words, the writer is saying: Don't let your imagination dwell on such a girl. To keep yourself safe, stay clear of her! You think you're too strong to fall for her wiles? Don't be too sure. Such girls leave a trail of so-called "strong men" who have found themselves weak when tempted.

"BLESSED IS THE MAN WHO WALKETH NOT IN THE COUNSEL OF THE UNGODLY, NOR STANDETH IN THE WAY OF SINNERS, NOR SITTETH IN THE SEAT OF THE SCORNFUL" (Psalm 1:1).

Where do you walk? Where do you stand? Where do you sit?

Does it matter? God's word promises blessing to the man who is careful not to walk in the wrong way, nor to stand in the wrong place, nor to sit with the wrong people! What does this mean? Let's take a look at "Pete" in our Training Manuals. First we have Pete the "Perambulator" . . . just walking by. Next, Pete the "Spectator" . . . standing to spy. Then, Pete the "Participator" . . . soon getting high.

Teacher: Consider together with your class these 3 cartoon sequences involving Pete. Discuss Pete's progressive behavior as follows:

How did Pete end up at the Dug Out instead of the church? Where did he go wrong? Since all action begins in the mind, let's play a "re-run" of Pete's "mind-track." Let's start in Scene 1 where Pete is deliberating about walking past the Dug Out. Here we find him telling himself, "No harm in walking by!"

No harm in walking by? Who do you suppose whispered that half-truth in his ear? Was it the Holy Spirit of God? Or an unholy spirit? What kind of counsel (or advice) was he heeding? Godly counsel or ungodly counsel?

Remember: "Blessed is the man who walketh not in the counsel of the ungodly." Because Pete wasn't on his guard against "ungodly counsel" from Satan, he swallowed this innocent-sounding line without a moment's hesitation. Pete the Perambulator "just walking by" (with his Bible in his hand) became Pete the Spectator "standing to spy" (with his Bible tucked into his hip pocket) . . . and at last, Pete the Participator "soon getting high!"

Though Satan often plants "ungodly counsel" in our minds through direct suggestions, he may plant thoughts in our minds through words from the lips of acquaintances and pals. On one occasion he tried to influence Jesus through Peter's lips (Matt. 16:22). Since he was brash enough to try this on the Son of God, can we hope to escape similar attacks? Our only defense is to learn how to recognize his "ungodly counsel."

GODLY OR UNGODLY COUNSEL?
(Page 28, Student's Training Manual)

To keep from walking "in the counsel of the ungodly," test the counsel against God's Word. If any part of it is not in agreement with God's Word, you may be sure it comes from the enemy! It is "ungodly" counsel! Reject it promptly! Godly counsel never goes against God's Word.

Have students (1) complete the scripture reference; (2) consider the advice given in the cartoon accompanying the reference, and (3) check whether or not the advice is "godly counsel" by testing the advice against God's Word.

WHAT DOES IT MEAN TO WALK "CIRCUMSPECTLY"?

Call attention to the illustration (at the bottom of the page) showing "wise Pete walking circumspectly."

How could Pete have known that the suggestion, "No harm in just walking by" was from the enemy? Because God's Word tells us to walk "circumspectly, not as fools, but as wise" (Eph. 5:15).

What does it mean to walk "circumspectly"? Let's break the word into its two main parts: "circum" and "spect." "Circum" means "around." In the word "circum-ference," for example, it refers to the outer edge of a circle. "Spect" means to behold, or observe, or watch. Therefore to walk "circum-spectly" in this world as a Christian is to (1) circle around temptations ... to take a round-about course ... to hug the outer edge (so as to keep as much distance as possible between you and the core of temptation) and (2) to keep watchful ... to walk with your eyes wide open!

Is this being cowardly? No! The Bible says this is being wise! "Walk circumspectly, not as fools, but as wise." The Bible says, "A wise man feareth and departeth from evil" (Prov. 14:16) while the fool is confident and cocky, walking right into it! Does it make any difference where you walk, stand, or sit? The Bible says "Enter not into the path of the wicked. Avoid it, pass not by it, turn from it" (Prov. 4:14,15). Yes, it does matter! To you — and to God!

Prayer:

Give us, Father, we pray, the necessary firmness of mind to discipline ourselves mentally, morally and physically so that we may stand straight and tall before the world and before you. As we walk through life, may we not walk as fools blindly following the crowd, but may we walk as wise men with our eyes open, staying on the one-way road that leads to a rewarding life in Christ Jesus. Amen.

Memory Question No. 4: What admonition should we consider when we decide which path in life to choose?

Answer: "Enter not into the path of the wicked, and go not in the way of evil men. Avoid it, pass not by it, turn from it and pass away" (Prov. 4:14,15).

IMPROVING YOUR FACE

(Pages 29 — 35, Student's Training Manual)

YOU WILL NEED: Safety razor, electric razor, various kinds of shaving creams and after-shaving lotions (if you choose to give a shaving demonstration).

If you wish to invite a barber in the community to be your "guest-expert" for this training period, select one who is refined in speech and manner. In choosing outside assistance, always give preference to those who share your beliefs concerning Christ.

HOW IMPORTANT IS YOUR FACE? PLENTY!

First of all, your face is important to God! No matter how ordinary it may appear to you, God can use it. You don't have to be handsome. You simply need to be so in tune with Jesus that you share his feelings and think his thoughts. When this happens **inside**, it shows on the **outside!** Your face becomes a living advertisement for him.

FACES CAN ATTRACT OTHERS TO JESUS

Young people today are searching faces. They're searching for someone who looks as though he's found the answer to life. What they're really seeking in a face is Jesus, for he is the way, the truth and the life (John 14:6). When a face reflects Jesus, it bears an unmistakable quality about it that sets it apart from the crowd. It's **alive and enthusiastic** — not hollow, empty and bored. It's **open and genuine** — not masked. **And it actually sheds forth a kind of radiance that attracts others.**

A "JESUS-SHINE" EXCITES CURIOSITY

When others see a fellow wearing a "Jesus-shine" on his face, they wonder, "What's his secret?" And they conclude, **"Whatever he's got, I need it too!"** They seek excuses to talk with that fellow in order to discover the secret behind his face. And when they do discover the secret, they've discovered Jesus! For it was Jesus' peace and love written all over that face that drew them in the first place!

And because they've seen Jesus in someone's face, they can no longer deny that he is real. Will they see him in your face? They can. **Your face can become a live exhibition of Jesus!**

YOUR FACIAL GROOMING AFFECTS THE MESSAGE

If your face is to be a good advertisement for Jesus, it must picture you at your best. An advertising billboard that is dilapidated "wipes out" the impact of its message. Likewise a face that is poorly groomed detracts from the message it should proclaim about the Saviour. Instead, a poorly groomed face can bring discredit to him. This fact alone is reason enough to give attention to the appearance of your face.

YOUR FACE CAN HARM YOUR OWN CAUSE, TOO!

If you neglect your facial appearance, you may harm your own cause — as well as Christ's cause — for your face is a powerful agent that can work either **for** you or **against** you. Some fellows think it's sissified for a guy to look in a mirror. (If someone catches them, they feel embarrassed.) **But mirrors are for men, too! Since everyone else looks at your face, you'd better find out what they are seeing!**

Why is your face an especially important part of you? Our Training Manuals give us four reasons.

1. YOU IDENTIFY YOURSELF WITH YOUR FACE.
(Page 29, Student's Training Manual)

Call students' attention to the "faceless snapshot." Read aloud the questions listed there. Have students check their responses.

If you've been sincere in your answers to these questions, undoubtedly you've checked all the "no" boxes, proving that your face does hold special significance. Why is this true? Because more than anything else, your face equals "you"! In your own mind, **you and your face are indivisible — identical!** Your face is the first place people look when they meet you. And when they're away from you, a mental vision of your face helps them to remember you! To sum it up — **your face is "you"!**

2. YOUR FACE IS AN "INFORMATION-GAP" FILLER.

Refer students to illustration showing back views of 3 heads.

If this were the only view you ever saw of these 3 fellows, would you feel hampered in getting to know them? **Yes — to a surprising degree!** Unconsciously you "read" another person's face to discover important personal information about him. If you were never able to see a person's face, what kinds of information would you lack concerning him?

Have your students list in their Training Manuals (page 29) 3 kinds of information a person's face communicates to others. Ask students to share their ideas. You may want to make a summary on the chalkboard as follows:

A person's face reveals information concerning . . .
1. His emotional state, his feelings and moods.
2. His basic disposition, his temperament and personality.
3. His health and vitality.

3. YOUR FACE AFFECTS OTHER PEOPLE

Let's say you're a newcomer to the area. To help you get acquainted, your mother suggests you invite one of the boys in your class for a backyard barbecue and a game of badminton. Which of the 3 boys pictured here would you select?

(Let the students offer their ideas.)

Do the 3 boys appear equally approachable and inviting? Hardly. The first boy looks dull and lifeless. (No fun to be with!) The second boy looks irritable and hard-headed. (Who'd want to spend time with him?) But the third boy looks pleasant, easy to get along with, alert and interested in life. **He's the one you'd probably choose to invite home.**

What does this tell you about the part a person's face plays in his social relationships?

Have students answer this question in space provided in their Training Manuals. Ask several to read their answers. Summarize on chalkboard as follows:

A fellow's face . . .
Has power to attract others.
Has power to repel others.
Can help him in his social relationships.
Can hinder him in his social relationships.
Can make him popular or unpopular.

4. YOUR FACE AFFECTS YOUR OPINION OF YOUR-SELF.

Because you identify "yourself" with your face, your feelings about your face greatly affect your "self-image." Psychologists say that a healthy self-image contributes toward successful behavior patterns. Change a man's face, they say, and invariably you change the man himself. Surgeons repeatedly have noted remarkable personality and behavior changes occurring in the lives of patients whose faces have been physically altered. Certainly an improved facial appearance will bring about increased self-confidence and self-esteem in any person.

Consider the boy shown in item No. 4. Obviously he is pleased with what he sees in the mirror. In the spaces provided, tell what happens when a fellow feels good about his face. Let the illustrations give you a clue.

Ask the students to share their answers. Summarize as follows:

When you feel good about what you see in the mirror . . .
(A) You face the world feeling good about yourself.
(B) Others respond to your attitude and feel good toward you, too!

ARE YOU SATISFIED WITH YOUR FACIAL APPEAR-ANCE?

If you're like most fellows, you'd probably like to change your face if you could. The surprising fact is that **you can!** Every boy, regardless of his features, can make himself a good face — and he doesn't need to visit a plastic surgeon to do it! Shakespeare wrote long ago, **"God has given you one face and you make yourself another."** How? We'll see.

THREE AREAS OF FACE-DEVELOPMENT THAT DEPEND ON YOU
(Page 30, Student's Training Manual)

How can you make yourself "another face"? *(Have students read from their Training Manuals concerning the 3 areas of face-development which are subject to their control.)*

WHAT CAN YOU DO TO MAKE "SKIN-DEEP" IMPROVEMENTS IN YOUR FACIAL APPEARANCE?
(Page 31, Student's Training Manual)

The boy pictured here has been overcome by 9 different "face-foes." But you don't need to be! There's an easy way to put every one of them on the run!

FACE FOE NO. 1 AND 2
(Muddy, sallow skin color; listless, dark-circled eyes.)

Both of these enemies can be conquered by simply following good health rules. The way you eat, exercise and sleep all show on your face. If you want clearer eyes, whiter teeth, fewer facial eruptions, improved skin tones and a healthier glow to your face — get plenty of fresh air and exercise, eat properly, drink lots of water, maintain good elimination and get sufficient sleep.

FACE FOE NO. 3
(Spotted, grease-smudged eyeglasses.)

Do eyeglasses spoil a boy's appearance? Clean glasses are never detrimental to a fellow's looks. (Many girls think boys look more masculine with glasses than without!) But dirty, smudged glasses will detract from even the most handsome face. Remember that others notice spots on your lenses more easily than you do; for you are focusing beyond the lenses, looking **through** them, not at them, as others do.

Clean your glasses regularly using water or eyeglass cleaner. Dry the lenses with a soft, clean cloth. When you put your glasses on or take them off, don't duck your head. This is an apologetic gesture. Hold your head up like a man! Wear your glasses confidently and they'll look sharp on you! Of course, you may want to consider contact lenses for other reasons. Consult your optometrist. He'll tell you if they are advisable.

FACE FOE NO. 4
(Food-encrusted, yellow teeth.)

Your best weapon against this enemy is the toothbrush. When caught without one, rinse your mouth after eating to wash away food particles lodged between your teeth.

Do you worry because your teeth are crooked? Clean, glistening teeth are far more important to your good looks than perfectly aligned ones. An imperfect tooth alignment usually registers in the minds of others as nothing more than "your special trademark" — and not the appearance defect you suspect.

If you must wear braces for an extreme alignment problem, don't try to hide your braces when you smile. If you cover them with your hands, you actually call more attention to them. Smile openly and smile often! Girls will notice the friendliness of your smile rather than your teeth braces. But remember . . . food-encrusted yellow teeth **will** be noticed and **will** detract from your smile.

FACE-FOES NO. 5, 6 and 7
(Crusted eyelids, matter in corner of eyes, dirty ears, grimy skin and dirt-clogged pores.)

All of these face-foes will yield to careful cleansing. Wash your face often and wash it well. Work up a sudsy lather in both hands and massage every inch of your face. Scrub around your hairline where perspiration and dust collect. To cleanse your eyes, wash away the crust or matter by wiping from the inside out. Get into the creases around your nose. Then splash-rinse, first with warm water and then with cold.

Your cleansing job doesn't end at the chin-line. A clean face demands a clean neck — and so does a clean shirt! And don't forget your ears. (Others look at them more easily than you do!) Drape a washcloth over your little finger and gently work around each fold. Get behind them, too!

FACE-FOE NO. 8
(Facial eruptions, pimples, bumps.)

This is a common facial foe that many teenagers must battle. Follow the steps listed in your Training Manuals and you'll put this enemy on the run.

Teacher: Discuss each one of the steps listed in the Student's Training Manual as follows:

Avoid pimple-producing foods.

During adolescence, your oil glands work overtime secreting oil into your pores. Add a greasy diet and your overloaded system sends up S.O.S. signals in the form of pimples. Their message? "Help! Lay off the fats! I've had all I can stand!" If this is your problem, avoid the pimple-producing foods listed in your Training Manuals.

Keep your face and scalp clean and free of oil.

An oily face provides a perfect breeding-ground for bacteria. Wash your face several times a day. You may want to use an antiseptic soap. Shampoo your hair often, too; for dirty, oily hair promotes pimples. Don't apply greasy hair lotion after your shampoo.

Maintain good bowel function.

Your skin plays a part in excreting waste. A sluggish elimination system can overburden your skin's role in this. Therefore drink plenty of water and eat enough vegetables and fresh fruit to provide normal roughage.

Keep your hands off your face.

Watch that urge to squeeze, dig or pick! Rather than helping the problem, an innocent "squeeze job" can aggravate it by spreading the infection beneath the skin to adjacent areas. If your fingers or nails are not clean, you invite bacterial infection, too. Don't risk a permanently scarred, pock-marked, pitted face. Keep your hands off!

Avoid emotional upsets.

Don't fret or panic over pimples (or anything else in your life), for emotional upsets trigger skin problems. Get sufficient rest and relaxing outdoor exercise to relieve tensions. Try spiritual sedatives, too. "In quietness and in confidence shall be your strength" (Isa. 30:15). Or, "All things work together for good to them that love God" (Rom. 8:28).

Consult a doctor.

If your skin problem is severe, consult a dermatologist. He can help you through this troublesome period as he has helped many others. Above all, don't bury your head in the sand and don't become a hideaway! An outbreak of pimples is no reason to avoid the human race. You are not alone in this problem. More than 85% of all teenagers suffer from it — and boys more severely than girls. Remember also, that other people — yes, girls too — enjoy the "real you" inside, not just your outer layer! You can have pimples and still be popular!

What's the difference between "Pimply Pete" and "Pimply Paul"?

Refer students to illustrations of "Pimply Pete" and "Pimply Paul," page 32, Student's Training Manual.

"Pimply Pete" is having a good time, and so is everyone around him. But not so with "Pimply Paul." What makes the difference?

Have students write their answers in Training Manuals, then discuss as follows:

"Pimply Pete's" philosophy is this: Forget your pimples and others will, too! "Pimply Paul," instead of forgetting his pimples, exaggerates them in his mind. He imagines his face has become a "disaster area" — and it does look like one! But it is not because of his pimples that it looks that way. It is because of the self-conscious fears and self-doubts that are registered on his face.

Of course, the kids avoid him! No one enjoys observing someone's embarrassed misery! Of course, they turn away. It's easier on them, and they hope they're making it easier on him too! But the simplest solution for all would be for Paul simply to put his pimples out of mind — to **remember** to **forget** them!

FACE-FOE NO. 9

(Patchy, scraggly whiskers.)

You may not be troubled with this face-foe yet; but sometime before you are 17, you'll discover fuzz on your chin and upper lip. In order to look well-groomed, you'll find it necessary to master the art of shaving. Your Training Manuals (page 32) offer tips to help you.

Teacher: You may wish to ask a local barber to show your students the various kinds of shaving products available and to demonstrate shaving skills. Or, you yourself can provide this demonstration.

Tip No. 1 — Determine the kind of cutting device that will work best on your beard.

Refer students to illustrations in their Training Manuals.

If your hair follicle is straight, your hair projects from the follicle in a straight line, and you can shave successfully with an electric shaver or a safety razor.
If your hair follicle is slanted or curved, your hair projects from the follicle in a slanted or curved line, oftentimes lying flat on your face. In this case, you can shave successfully with a safety razor, but success with an electric shaver is not so certain. Don't give up too soon, however, for results may improve with continued usage.

If the safety razor proves to be your best choice, you'll want to learn how to use it properly.

Tip No. 2 — Pull your safety razor with — not against — the lay of your whiskers (if your whiskers grow slanted or curved).

If you cut against the lay of your whiskers, you can expect rashy, pimply skin. Why? As you see in the diagram in your Training Manual the pressure of the blade forces the whisker to protrude from its follicle so completely that the hair is cut off below the follicle opening. As the surrounding skin relaxes, it closes over the top of the shortened whisker, sealing it off, and later producing a pimple as a result of the "ingrown hair."

To avoid this, pull your razor in the same direction that your whiskers grow. This leaves the cut whisker protruding slightly above the follicle opening. Result? No trouble from "ingrown hairs"!

Tip No. 3 — Determine your individual shaving pattern.
(Page 33, Student's Training Manual)

When whiskers first appear, you may shave only once a week. Later however, shaving will become a daily task — and one which you'll want to perform as quickly as possible. Repeating the same basic shaving pattern each time you shave will expedite the operation.

To discover your proper pattern, first determine the direction your whiskers grow. To do this, rub your hand over your whiskers first in one direction, then the other. The direction that feels smoother to your hand is the direction your whiskers grow and the proper direction to pull your blade.

Have your students complete their personal shaving pattern chart on page 33, Student's Training Manual.

Tip No. 4 — Develop proper cutting techniques to prevent nicks and cuts.

Before you begin to shave, steam your face for several minutes, using a hot, moist towel. Then apply a soapy lather to your face, using either shaving soap, tube cream or an aerosol type cream. Warm your shaver under hot water; check to make sure the blade is tight. Then start your shaving operation using short, light strokes.

Don't side-slip the blade! This can cause a nasty nick! Always pull the razor in the same direction that the handle is pointing. *(Refer students to illustration in Student's Training Manual.)* If you nick yourself, stop the bleeding with a styptic pencil. Apply a small patch of tissue to absorb the blood.

When finished shaving, unclamp the blade slightly and twirl the razor under running hot water to rinse away clogged whiskers and cream. Shake it and lay it out to dry. If your skin is tender or dry, an after-shave lotion will help smoothe and lubricate it. If your skin is oily, apply cologne. This acts as an astringent.

Is a moustache or beard the answer?

Because your face is still tender and the tendency toward skin eruptions is greater during your teens, your early years of shaving will be your roughest. You may even wonder, "Why not let my whiskers grow?" At this stage of your development your whiskers are likely to be patchy. With gaps of skin showing here and there, you may even resemble a molting chicken!

Some grown men never develop the solid growth of whiskers necessary to form a good-looking beard or moustache. If you should manage to grow one, keep it trimmed neatly. When a moustache projects below the upper lip into the mouth area, it presents a distasteful appearance — especially when contaminated with food.

Before growing a beard or moustache, you must also take into consideration the fact that some people react negatively to them. If by wearing a beard you realize a very definite improvement of appearance, you will receive greater acceptance.

WHAT CAN YOU DO TO MAKE "MUSCLE-DEEP" IMPROVEMENTS IN YOUR FACIAL APPEARANCE?
(Page 33, Student's Training Manual.)

To make "muscle-deep" improvements in your facial appearance, discipline the corners of your mouth, discipline your jaw muscles, and discipline your eyelids. A slouchy "facial posture" can ruin your manly appearance as quickly as a slouchy body posture. Check yourself in a mirror from time to time. Try to catch yourself in an unguarded moment. You may be surprised at the unbecoming facial habits you practice.

Have your students place check marks in the squares in answer to the three facial questionnaires. Make comments as follows:

Discipline the corners of your mouth.

No man looks masterful when he appears "down in the mouth." To correct any tendency toward a droopy mouth, train yourself to maintain a light upturn at the corners. This doesn't mean you must wear a habitual grin, but a deadpan face does nothing for your looks either!

If you want to give your popularity a boost, cultivate a friendly, optimistic expression. Don't be stingy with your smiles either. And after you've flashed a smile, retain a trace of it permanently. **First choice everywhere is the boy who looks pleasant!**

Discipline your jaw muscles.

A gaping mouth makes a boy look stupid and spiritless. Show the world you have enough backbone and grit to keep your mouth closed and your jaws in place. Keeping your mouth closed is a good health habit also, for it prevents unfiltered air from contaminating your lungs.

If you've inherited a heavy, protruding lower lip, you'll need to discipline your jaw muscles even more carefully. A hanging jaw allows your heavy lower lip to roll out loosely, making it protrude even more and giving your entire face a sullen, pouty expression. To overcome a thick, pouchy lower lip, deliberately maintain a slight smile. This "horizontal stretch" elongates the lip and makes it appear thinner.

Discipline your eyelids.

Don't let your eyelids droop at half mast! Staring through half-open eyes makes a fellow look languid and insipid. Snap your eyes wide open so you'll look like a real man — full of stamina and vigor! If this is hard work, you may need more sleep!

WHAT CAN YOU DO TO MAKE "SOUL-DEEP" IMPROVEMENTS IN YOUR FACIAL APPEARANCE?
(Page 34, Student's Training Manual)

To completely eradicate bad facial expressions involves more than changing your muscle-habits. It involves changing your inner thought-habits as well. Your thoughts and feelings spring from deep within. Therefore they must be changed from deep within.

The countenance is the "cardiogram of the heart."

If you want to present a good face to the world, let God control your heart. There's no such thing as a good-looking guy with an ugly heart! If ugly thoughts fill a young man's mind, ugly expressions stamp themselves on his face.

You have heard the expression, "The eyes are the mirror of the soul." But did you ever consider that the **countenance** can also be called the **"cardiogram of the heart"**? Your facial muscles are like sensitive cardiograph instruments registering every minute change in the character of your heart.

Your face is also like the "print-out" of a computer.

Your facial muscles constantly reveal the inner man. Like a computer "print-out" they send out information concerning the contents of your "in-put" storage center" (your heart). Every secret thought, every imagination, every feeling, every inner motive, every attitude, every emotional response that you allow to enter your "in-put storage center" is disclosed upon your face as a "print-out" for all to read! It's just as the verse says:

"The false, the deceit that you bear in your heart
 Will not stay inside where it first got a start,
 For sinew and blood are a thin veil of lace . . .
 What you wear in your heart, you wear in your face!"
                                        —(Author unknown)

Let's look at the three fellows in our Training Manuals (page 34 and 35) to see what happens to their facial "print-outs" when various kinds of heart "in-puts" are allowed.

HEART "IN-PUT" AND FACIAL "PRINT-OUT" NO. 1

Here we have a young man filled with negative, destructive thoughts toward others. What has happened to his face?

His lips have formed harsh, surly lines.
His jaws are clamped together.
His facial muscles have become rigid.
His eyes are narrowed into thin slits.
His brow has formed a deep scowl.

His appearance is at its worst! And the more frequently he allows such attitudes to make this kind of "print-out" on his countenance, the more permanent the facial damage will become. This guy hates others and shows it on his face!

Let's look into the "In-put Storage Center" of his "Inner Life and Heart" to see what kinds of thoughts he's allowed to enter there.

Divide the class into two sections — one to read the Heart "In-put" and the other to follow with the corresponding Facial "Print-Out." Have the students read alternately.

HEART "IN-PUT" AND FACIAL "PRINT-OUT" NO. 2

This sad-looking character has negative, destructive thoughts, also. But they are not directed toward others; they're directed toward himself. He lacks self-confidence. He's full of timidity and self-doubts. He has no optimism . . . no courage. Why? Because he knows he has done wrong things.

The Bible says a clear conscience makes a fellow as bold as a lion, but a guilty conscience makes him flee even when no one is pursuing him! (See Prov. 28:1.) Because this fellow has ceased to respect himself, his expression has become masked and guarded, his eyes evasive, and the light has gone out of his face.

His facial muscles, responding to his uneasy heart and mind, have produced a strained, apologetic appearance which instinctively repels others. Because this fellow's face shows he is ill at ease within himself, other kids feel ill at ease around him, too — and there goes his popularity!

Let's look into the "In-Put Storage Center" of his "Inner Life and Heart" to see what kinds of thoughts he's allowed to enter there.

(Have students read alternately as on No. 1.)

Eventually the "Print-out" will appear.

Some of you may be thinking, "I know boys who hate others and have plenty to feel guilty about, but they don't look like these two guys. How are they getting off so easy?"

They aren't! The effects may be delayed, but eventually the marks will appear on their faces. Seeds do not sprout through the ground overnight. They remain hidden in the dark for a time, but eventually make their way to the surface and to the light.

It's the same way with sin. God's Word says, "Be sure your sin will find you out" (Num. 32:23). "Be not deceived; God is not mocked; for whatsoever a man soweth, that shall he also reap" (Gal. 6:7). What a person sows in his heart, he'll reap in his face — as well as in his life.

God has written in his Word, "The shew of their countenance doth witness against them; and they declare their sin . . . they hide it not" (Isa. 3:9). No one can fool the computer and avoid the tell-tale "print-out"!

God can give you a new "In-put" and a new "Out-put."

Is there a way out? Yes! You can let God transform your heart — and your face! You can let him remove the destructive attitudes you harbor toward others and the guilt and reproach you feel toward yourself!

God says, "A new heart also will I give you, and a new spirit will I put within you" (Ezek. 36:26). "Therefore if any man be in Christ, he is a new creature: old things are passed away; behold, all things are become new" (2 Cor. 5:17).

You can become a brand new person with a new kind of "in-put." New thoughts, new desires, new motives for living, new responses to situations — a new attitude toward life, toward others and toward yourself! This new "in-put" reveals itself in a new "print-out" as we see in our third illustration.

HEART "IN-PUT" AND FACIAL "PRINT-OUT" NO .3
(Page 35, Student's Training Manual)

Let's look into this fellow's "In-put Storage Center" to discover what kinds of thoughts he has stored there.

Apparently this fellow has been storing God's Word in his heart, for all of his thoughts appear to be in agreement with it. Let's check to see if this is true.

(Assign the following scripture references to be read aloud with the corresponding "input-thoughts:"

Input (1) — Phil. 4:13	*Input (5) — Rom. 8:28*
Input (2) — 1 Cor. 6:20	*Input (6) — Eph. 4:32*
Input (3) — Heb. 12:14	*Input (7) — 1 Tim. 5:22b*
Input (4) — 1 Jn. 1:9	*Input (8) — Heb. 13:6*

What kind of facial "print-out" did these positive and powerful thoughts from God's Word produce? They are listed for us at the bottom of page 35. Peace, fearlessness, freedom from guilt, self-esteem, purity, a forgiving spirit, self-confidence, and optimism. Now, let's see if we can determine which of the 8 "in-puts" produced each of the 8 "facial print-outs." Can you tie them together in pairs? Enter the appropriate "print-out" in the space provided.

Note: This exercise will further impress the students with the impact of God's Word stored in the heart and mind. Answers are:

1 — Self-confidence	*5 — Optimism*
2 — Self-esteem	*6 — A forgiving spirit*
3 — Peace	*7 — Purity*
4 — Freedom from guilt	*8 — Fearlessness*

Confession restores and renews the face.

Some of you may be wondering, "What happens if I yield to my old nature again after receiving this brand new heart? What if I allow some of the old "in-put" to enter again?

God has provided a way to cleanse your heart and renew your face — confession and restitution! King David prayed, "Wash me throughly from mine iniquity and cleanse me from my sin . . . create in me a clean heart, O God."

If your words or actions have harmed others, God may want you to say "I'm sorry" to those you've harmed. He may want you to make restitution. Whatever he tells you to do, obey him. This is God's way for you to regain self-respect and peace. With complete confession and forgiveness, the guilt and reproach are lifted from your heart — and from your face!

God forgives sex sins, too.

Some boys find it hard to believe that God will forgive their sins concerning sex. But if you look into King David's life, you'll discover that the forgiveness he desired from God in Psalm 51 was for this type of sin. Did God forgive him? Listen to David's words:

"Blessed is he whose transgression is forgiven, whose sin is covered. When I kept silence, my bones waxed old through my roaring all day long. For day and night thy hand was heavy upon me . . . I said, I will confess my transgressions unto the Lord; and thou forgavest the iniquity of my sin."

A word of warning . . .

God forgave David, and he offers the same forgiveness to every person who turns from his sin, determining not to take that route again. But let's not forget this fact: Though David sensed peace and joy in God's forgiveness, yet he suffered trouble in his life as a result of his sin.

The Bible says, "Can a man take fire in his bosom, and his clothes not be burned" (Prov. 6:27)? When temptation to sin seems attractive, we need to remember that fire, also, is attractive. But fire burns! And the burns can leave lifelong scars.

Sex sins muddy the very fountain of a man's life — that part of his being that holds tremendous power, the capacity to generate new life. "Keep thyself pure" (1 Tim. 5:22b), and keep your face alive with the joy of living!

The shine on your face speaks for you!

Sometimes the "Jesus-shine" on a man's face is so apparent that his face actually appears to glow with an inner light.

When Stephen, the first Christian martyr, was brought before the council, his accusers saw the light shining forth in his face. The Bible tells us that "all that sat in the council, looking steadfastly on him, saw his face as it had been the face of an angel" (Acts 6:15). **What a "print-out"!**

Paul S. Rees says, "A bored face is the badge of a bogus Christianity . . . a radiant face is its authentic signature. A true story illustrates this point:

A bishop while speaking in the huge auditorium at Moody Church in Chicago many years ago, developed sudden laryngitis and could not make himself heard. At the close of the message a man made his way to the front to speak to the bishop. "Sir," he said, "I sat tonight where I could not hear a word of your sermon, but I could not escape the shine on your face! If to believe the gospel means the coming of a light such as I saw on your face, I want to confess Christ as my Savior!"

The "man in demand" presents a good face to the world as a witness to Jesus Christ. You can be such a man!

Prayer:

Father, we come to you with our ordinary-looking faces, but we know you can use them as "living advertisements" for you. Help us to have faces that might not detract from our Christian witness. May our attitudes and thoughts be those that will allow our faces to reflect the glory of your Son, Jesus Christ, so that others may be drawn to Him as their Savior, too. Amen.

Memory Question No. 5: Can we continually sow ugly thoughts in our minds and hearts without eventually reaping the consequences on our faces and in our lives?

Answer: "Be not deceived; God is not mocked: for whatsoever a man soweth, that shall he also reap" (Gal. 6:7).

MANAGING YOUR HAIR
(Pages 36 — 41, Student's Training Manual)

PRIOR TO CLASS: Determine whether or not you will invite a local barber or hair-stylist to be your guest-expert for this session to give the students advice regarding hair care and hair styling.

If not, you may wish to bring to class various kinds of hair care items (such as brushes, combs, blowers, or various kinds of shampoos, lotions or sprays) to add interest to your teaching period or to use for actual demonstrations.

Use your own judgment in regard to this. Even without these visual aids, your students will be keenly interested in this teaching; for although boys are reluctant to admit it, they are vitally interested in the appearance of their hair.

IS YOUR HAIR REALLY IMPORTANT?
(Page 36, Student's Training Manual)

God has provided you with 120,000 hairs on your head. Does it matter what kind of care you give them? Is your hair really important, or is it simply a subject to "split hairs" over?

In our first cartoon on page 36 of the Training Manual, we find a frowzy-looking young man declaring that hair doesn't matter — **only what's inside really counts!** Do you agree with him? Is his viewpoint valid?

(Let your student express their opinions. Some may voice agreement.)

THE OUTER REVEALS THE INNER

Granted, what's inside your head is important! But if the **inside** is important, then the **outside** is, too, for the very reason that the outside normally expresses what's inside!

Psychiatrists, as well as human behavioral experts, have long known that **what goes on inside a man's head inevitably shows up on the outside!** For example, when a patient in a mental hospital begins to comb his hair, psychiatrists judge this to be a sign that he's improving mentally. Their conclusion is based on the inescapable law: **"The inner is forever becoming the outer."**

Even the animal kingdom displays this truth (as we see in our next cartoon). When an animal ceases to lick its hair into place, letting it become matted and dirty, a veterinarian judges this to be an outward sign of some inner ailment.

Is it illogical then for people to judge a fellow to be sick also — perhaps in his psyche, if not physically — when they observe him walking down the street with dirty, straggling, uncombed hair?

IS YOUR HAIR "JUST HAIR" . . . OR IS IT SOMETHING MORE?

The primary function of hair is simply to cover the head. Historically, however, hair has been **more than "just hair."** In various cultures and at different times a person's hair has symbolized important factors concerning his status in life.

One of the identifying marks of a convict, for example, was his shaved head. Likewise, for a woman's head to be shaved was considered a badge of personal disgrace. In China the pigtail traditionally signified servitude. In Bible times the uncut hair of the Nazarite was an outward emblem of his total consecration to God. When the days of his vow came to an end, the Nazarite shaved his head and placed his hair cuttings on the fire along with a sacrifice offered to God.

Even today people regard hair as a significant clue to other factors concerning the individual. Hair is still more than "just hair"! Our Training Manuals list 7 functions hair performs today.

(Have your students read and discuss these 7 functions briefly, then continue as follows:)

PEOPLE ADMIRE GOOD-LOOKING HAIR!

Since your hair does all these things for you, perhaps you should do something for it. Like keeping it well-groomed, perhaps?

Don't be misled. People are **not** indifferent to the way you wear your hair! The human mind is equipped with "eyes" that are instinctively artistic! The human eye readily perceives what looks good and what doesn't! **It appreciates cleanliness! It likes harmony! It responds to order!**

The same set of eyes that admires a sleek, curry-combed coat of hair on a horse also admires a clean, well-combed head of hair on a boy. **And who doesn't want to be admired?** Every normal fellow does! Fortunately it takes less effort for a fellow to groom the hair on his head than to groom the hair on a horse!

HOW DO YOU GROOM YOUR HAIR?
(Page 37, Student's Training Manual)

BRUSH YOUR HAIR!

One way to groom your hair is to brush it regularly. Will brushing really do anything for your hair? The experts say "yes!"

"If a young fellow will just brush his hair **regularly**," they say, "he'll see some **handsome hair!**" Here are 4 reasons they give:

1. Brushing will sweep out dust and dirt.

Do you realize how much dust your hair holds? Make this test: Shake your hair vigorously in a bright beam of light. Then step back quickly and take a look at the dust-laden whirlwind you've set in motion.

The thousands of hairs on your head provide a built-in dust-catcher and dirt-trap as efficient as any inventor could conceive! The hairs on your head also make a wonderful catch-all for smoke, soot and every other particle that floats through the air — from pillow feathers to pollen! If you want hair that's really clean, sweep away this foreign debris daily.

What kind of hair brush should you use? If your hair is thin and fine, a soft bristle brush will do. If your hair is heavy, choose stiffer bristles that will brush through to the scalp.

2. Brushing will add gloss to your hair.

If you want handsome plumage, take a lesson from the birds. They polish their feathers by preening them with their beaks, pulling from the roots to the tip ends. Of course, you don't have a beak like a bird, but you do have a hairbrush. As you sweep your brush along the strands of your hair, you polish and lubricate the entire length of the hair shaft, you spread oil from the scalp to the dry tips, and with every stroke you add a good-looking gloss to your hair!

3. Brushing will stimulate the scalp.

Don't tolerate a sluggish scalp! Why not? Because a sluggish scalp will never produce a healthy crop of hair! Brushing peps up the circulation and sends a flow of blood rushing to the roots of your hair. To be effective, your brushing must be vigorous and deep. You can't slide the bristles of your brush over the surface of your hair (like a skier gliding atop the snow) and expect to awaken a sluggish scalp.

Press the bristles firmly into your scalp, then lift your hair away from your scalp as you sweep the bristles upward and outward. Start at the back of your neck, then work around your entire head until your scalp feels alive and tingly all over.

4. Brushing will help control dandruff.

What causes that annoying scaly-white scurf to appear on your scalp? An outbreak of dandruff could indicate either that you've been neglecting the general rules of health and cleanliness or that your scalp is getting insufficient nourishment. Here's where your hairbrush can help you. When you massage your scalp (either with your hairbrush or your fingertips) you're increasing the blood circulation to your scalp — and with added blood circulation comes added nourishment.

If dandruff is a problem, do this: Every morning or night lower your head over the washbasin and give your hair a good shaking. Use your hairbrush to scratch loose the scales from your scalp. Don't injure or bruise your scalp but try to remove as much dandruff as possible. Your scalp needs to be free of this scurf to allow your hair follicles to breathe. And, of course, when you have a dandruff problem, wash your hair at least twice a week.

KEEP YOUR HAIRBRUSH CLEAN

When you've finished your daily hairbrushing, remove the loose hairs which cling to the brush by running your comb through the bristles. Comb back and forth several times in several directions so that no accumulation of loose hairs or lint remains trapped at the base of the bristles.

To wash your brush, swish it back and forth in warm, soapy water; give it a shake, then lay it — bristles downward — upon a towel to dry. Many hair specialists say the most important asset a teenage boy can possess in his hairbrush. Treat it with **respect!**

To review these pointers have your students complete the items under "Brush Your Hair" at the top of page 37. When completed, the reasons given should read:

1. To sweep away <u>dust</u> and <u>dirt</u>, etc.
2. To spread <u>oil</u> from the <u>scalp</u> (or roots) to the dry tips.
3. To give the scalp a stimulating <u>massage</u> to increase the circulation of <u>blood</u> to the scalp.
4. To help control <u>dandruff</u>.

WASH YOUR HAIR!

To groom your hair you must not only brush it, you must also wash it! How often should you wash your hair? If you don't want hair that looks like a floor-mop the janitor forgot to wash out, wash it **often enough to keep it really clean!** How often is "often enough"? It all depends.

Do you have an oily scalp?

If you have oily scalp (and many teenagers do because of overactive oil glands), then you'll want to wash your hair 2 to 3 times a week.

"But that sounds like a lot of work!" you say. Perhaps. But remember that keeping your hair clean will also help you have a better complexion! Oily, dirty hair clinging to your forehead or to the back of your neck provides a first-class breeding place for those pimples you detest!

Do you have a dry scalp?

If you have dry scalp, you may be able to go one week between scrubbings. Keep your schedule flexible, however, for other factors such as sports activities or your work-life may affect it.

Let's say, for instance, that you work all day in the hot sun shovelling dirt or coal, and the dust mingles with your perspiration to clog the pores on your scalp. You'll want to give your head a prompt scrubbing not only so you'll look and feel clean but also to get rid of scalp "build-up" and to allow your hair follicles to breathe normally again.

Generally speaking, however, you'll know it's time to wash your hair when certain warning signals appear.

(Have your students consider the warning signals described and illustrated in their Training Manuals.)

HERE'S THE WAY TO WASH YOUR HAIR

Like any other job in life, there's a **right way** and a **wrong way** to perform it! Nine steps toward a clean head of hair are listed in your Training Manuals. Test yourself. Can you place the 9 steps in proper sequence?

Give your students time to draw connecting lines between each hair-washing step and its proper sequence number. Correct and discuss as follows:

Step 1 — Brush your hair.

This is to loosen the dandruff and dirt on your scalp.

Step 2 — Drench with warm water.

Wet your hair thoroughly. Washing your hair beneath the shower makes this step easier. Adjust the temperature of the water-spray before you begin.

Step 3 — Apply liquid shampoo.

Don't skimp here! Use enough shampoo to work up a thick lather. What kind should you use? It depends upon the condition of your scalp and hair. Read the label to see what the manufacturer claims. Then give the shampoo a fair testing period so you can judge the results for yourself. The right shampoo can make a big difference in your hair. If you're troubled with dandruff, try a shampoo that is especially designed to combat the problem.

Step 4 — Lather-massage and rinse lightly.

Get in there and rub! Use all your fingers! Massage energetically, back and forth, around and around, until every inch of your scalp has been scrubbed. Then rinse away the soap.

Step 5 — Lather-massage and rinse thoroughly.

Your **first** lathering cuts away the surface oil. Your **second** lathering gives a deep-down cleansing. Make this final rinse a thorough one to flush away any trace of dulling soap film.

Step 6 — Towel-dry your hair.

Grab a thick turkish towel, drape it over your head and rub your hair until all excess moisture is removed.

Step 7 — Comb out snarls and tangles.

These are easier to remove while your hair is still damp. Start with the ends of your hair, then work toward your scalp.

Step 8 — Air dry your hair.

You can either let your hair dry naturally or use a blower.

Step 9 — Brush your hair.

When your hair is completely dry, give it another good brushing to replenish the oil from your scalp.

Now look in the mirror! You'll see a fellow with a fine head of clean hair, and one who has improved his appearance **100%!**

COMB YOUR HAIR
(Page 38, Student's Training Manual)

To groom your hair you must not only brush it and wash it, you must also comb it! The greater the length of your hair, the more easily it becomes tangled and the more important your comb becomes!

A tangle of anything — whether it be twine, barbed wire or hair — presents a disturbing picture. Tangles signify confusion. God is a God of order. His first act in creation was to produce order out of chaos. Your comb will help you do this for your hair, too.

When hairs lie approximately parallel to each other, they're "in order." When hairs lie in a crisscross manner, they're not in order. With one quick sweep of your comb you can capture those disheveled, crossed strands and lay them out in orderly, parallel paths. That's the purpose of your comb — to perform the final smooth-up job on your hair!

COMMON COURTESIES IN "COMB CONDUCT"

Give your students a few minutes to read the 4 rules of "comb conduct" listed in their Training Manuals. Have them write their ideas regarding the reasons for these rules. Discuss their answers as follows:

1. Don't ask to borrow your friend's comb. Why not?

This rule is for your protection as well as his. Infectious diseases may be transmitted in this way.

2. Don't comb your hair at the table. Why not?

Stray hairs and dandruff may float through the air. If your hair should land on your "date's" plate, you won't make a hit with her!

3. Try not to comb your hair in public. Why not?

The general rule of etiquette is that under normal circumstances your personal grooming should be conducted in private. If you get caught in a stiff breeze, however, it's better to straighten your hair than to look ungroomed throughout the occasion. But try to do the touch-up job as quickly and inconspicuously as possible.

4. Don't let your comb become dirty. Why not?

Keep your comb clean not only for the sake of personal hygiene but also for the sake of others who might view it. A dirty comb is a repulsive sight! Don't inflict it upon your friends or family. Girls are especially displeased to see a boy pull a cruddy, gummy comb out of his hip pocket and run it through his hair.

To clean your comb, use a soapy fingernail brush. Scrub through the comb's teeth with an outward motion starting at the base and brushing through to the outer edge.

HOW TO CHOOSE A HAIR STYLE THAT MAKES YOU LOOK YOUR BEST

Is your hair an asset or a detriment to your appearance? If your hair style is so bizarre that it attracts undue attention, it detracts from you as a person.

This does not mean that you cannot wear your hair in an individualized style. Your barber can shape, taper and blend your hair to give you a good-looking cut that's just right for you. The secret is to have a hair style that is personalized yet not so different as to be eye-stopping. **Moderation is the key.**

"Well," you say, "I think my hair style looks O.K., but **how can I know for sure?**" Here are 4 tests that a hair style must pass if it is to be an asset to a fellow's appearance:

(1) It must complement the shape of his face.
(2) It must complement his facial profile.
(3) It must complement his body stature.
(4) It must make him look masculine.

DOES YOUR HAIR STYLE COMPLEMENT YOUR FACIAL CONTOUR?
(Page 38, Student's Training Manual)

Faces, like potatoes and peanuts, come in all shapes and sizes. Your face may be basically round. The next guy's may be more square or oblong. The human eye, however, judges the oval (or "egg-shaped") face to be the most perfect.

"Great!" you say, "But what can I do about the bony structure of my face? It's here to stay!" Agreed. You can't squish in your cheek bones or flatten out your chin as you might reshape a soft ball of clay. But by rearranging your hair, you can make your face **appear** to have a more desirable contour. Like a magician, **you can fool the eye!** This is how you do it.

(Refer students to illustrations, pages 38 and 39 in Training Manuals.)

IS YOUR FACE LONG AND NARROW?

Your oblong face will appear more oval if you wear your hair flat on top with fullness added at the sides. Hair worn over the forehead helps shorten your face, too.

Never accentuate the vertical lines of your face by wearing long sideburns. A center part should also be avoided, since it appears as another vertical line to the eye. Try a low side part instead.

Never draw your hair away from your forehead or wear it high on your head as this would only add more length to your face.

IS YOUR FACE ROUND AND FULL?

You can make your circular face appear more oval by giving your hair an upward lift at the top of your head, while smoothing your hair flat and close to the sides, leaving your ears exposed. To break up the perfect circle pattern of your face, draw your hair higher on one side than the other, or cover one side of your forehead with hair. A diagonal part also helps to eliminate the symmetrical roundness of your face.

Never wear your hair flat on top or with fullness at the sides either above or below the ears. This would give you a plump "pumpkin face"! Do not add width to your cheeks by covering your ears. Avoid a center part.

IS YOUR JAW-LINE HEAVY AND YOUR FOREHEAD NARROW?

Add fullness above the temple and above the ears to balance the width of your jaw-line. A hair style that allows hair to cover your forehead is also good. (This adds fullness to your brow and at the same time conceals the narrowness of your forehead.)

Avoid wearing your hair flat and smooth at the temple or full at the jaw-line. Never fully expose the narrowness of your forehead.

IS YOUR FOREHEAD BROAD AND YOUR CHIN-LINE NARROW?

Camouflage the width of your forehead by drawing your hair down over one side of the forehead. Never add fullness at the temples. Try not to expose all of your forehead. Use a diagonal part instead of a center part.

IS YOUR FACE SQUARE?

You can make it appear more oval by lifting your hair at the top of your head to add height and drawing your hair close to the sides to minimize width. Don't cover your ears with bulky hair. (This would add width.) Hair drawn over one side of your forehead will help to break up the square, balanced pattern of your face. A diagonal part will also help this.

Avoid wearing your hair flat on top or full at the sides. Also avoid full broad bangs. These styles tend to emphasize the square, angular appearance of your face, as does a center part.

DO YOUR EARS PROTRUDE MORE THAN AVERAGE?

Be careful not to flatten your hair close to your head directly above your ears. Instead allow fullness there to camouflage the distance between the outer tip of your ears and the sides of your head.

DOES YOUR HAIR STYLE COMPLEMENT YOUR FACIAL PROFILE?
(Page 40, Student's Training Manual)

You are not always face-to-face with the world. The profile of your face is often on display. The wrong hair style can emphasize any disproportionate features you may have, whereas the proper hair style can counter-balance these problem features to give you a more pleasing profile.

IS YOUR NOSE LONG AND PROTRUDING?

Don't draw your hair back from your forehead. This will make your nose appear longer. Instead, allow some hair to protrude over your forehead to balance your protruding nose.

On the other hand, if your nose is small and flat, drawing your hair back away from your forehead will give it more prominence.

DO YOU HAVE A SLANTED, RECEDING FOREHEAD?

Compensate for a slanting brow by drawing your hair forward over your forehead.

DO YOU HAVE A HIGH FOREHEAD?

Conceal the height of your forehead by drawing your hair over it. Do not draw your hair straight back to fully expose your forehead.

DO YOU HAVE A PROMINENT, PROTRUDING FOREHEAD?

Keep your hair flat and smooth over your full forehead. Don't emphasize a bulging forehead with a bulky mass of hair.

DOES YOUR HAIR STYLE COMPLEMENT YOUR STATURE?

(Bottom of page 40, Student's Training Manual)

To be visually pleasing, your hair style must be compatible with your body proportions.

ARE YOU TALL?

Make certain your hair has enough fullness to dispel any "pinheaded" appearance.

ARE YOU HEAVY?

A bulky hair style adds heaviness to your appearance. Keep your hair neatly trimmed and your hair style moderate in size.

ARE YOU SHORT?

Do not let a huge head of hair overpower you. Your hair style should be in keeping with your diminutive size.

DOES YOUR HAIR STYLE MAKE YOU LOOK MASCULINE?
(Page 41, Student's Training Manual)

The human eye is accustomed to categorizing human beings **instantly** as either male or female! When it cannot do this, frustration and displeasure result. If a boy's hair style is such that it confuses his sex identity, it registers as a negative feature and becomes a discredit to him.

A PUMPKIN THAT LOOKS LIKE A SQUASH IS A CULL

When a farmer chooses a pumpkin to display at the fair, he bypasses any that deviate from the normal pattern. He knows that the slightest confusion regarding species would be considered a demerit. To be a first-class specimen, a mature pumpkin must look exactly like a pumpkin! If it's not quickly distinguishable from a squash, it's classified a "cull."

A FIRST-CLASS MAN MUST LOOK LIKE A MAN

Likewise, to be a prime specimen of a man, a fellow at maturity must be quickly distinguishable as a male. If his hair style adds confusion in regard to his sex, it becomes a demerit. To look his best, a fellow must look like a guy — not a girl! His hair style must tell the world exactly what he is!

(Call students' attention to cartoon, page 41, Student's Training Manuals.)

THE SCRIPTURAL BASIS FOR MAINTAINING SEX IDENTITY
(Page 41, Student's Training Manual)

As you discuss the following 5 points, call upon various students to read aloud from their Training Manuals the pertinent scripture verses included under each point.

1. TWO SEXES, NOT ONE.

How should a Christian look upon "uni-sex" — the blurring of the sexes into one? According to the Bible, a world composed of **one sex** is not what God had in mind!

(A student may read Gen. 1:27.)

"Male and female created He them." Notice the **"and."** Male **and** female — not **one,** but two separate sexes! And isn't the "other" sex referred to as the "opposite" sex rather than the **"similar"** sex? The word "opposite" means "set in contrast one to the other" — the very opposite of "similar"! "Masculinity" likewise is defined as the **opposite** of feminity.

2. WOMAN TAKEN "OUT OF" MAN.

The word "woman" means "taken **out of** man."

(A student may read Gen. 2:22, 23)

"And the rib, which the LORD GOD had taken from man, made he a woman, and brought her unto the man. And Adam said, This is now bone of my bones, and flesh of my flesh: she shall be called Woman, because she was taken out of Man." **Since God took "femininity" out of man, why try to frustrate his puposes by attempting to put it back in again?**

3. DRESS AND HAIR STYLES TO DIFFER.

According to scripture, God wants us to maintain a distinction between the sexes in our outward appearance. He wants girls to look like girls, and boys to look like boys! And doesn't that make sense? Otherwise confusion would reign! God wants a man to be easily distinguishable from a woman, even at a distance, by the way he dresses and wears his hair.

(A student may read Deut. 22:5 and 1 Cor. 11:14.)

"The woman shall not wear that which pertaineth unto a man, neither shall a man put on a woman's garment: for all that do so are an abomination unto the LORD thy God."

"Doth not even nature itself teach you, that, if a man have long hair, it is a shame unto him?"

Customs change but the principle remains.

"But," you might ask, "what about the periods when men wore rather long hair?" True, customs change from one era to another. But no matter what the standard hair length for men may be from time to time, a man's hair, by comparison, is always to be shorter than a woman's.

"Why can't it be the other way around?" you might ask. "Wouldn't it be just as easy to distinguish a man from a woman if all men wore their hair long and all women wore their hair short?" True. A woman's long hair, however, serves a purpose other than simply identifying her as a woman.

4. A WOMAN'S HAIR IS A "HEAD COVERING" SYMBOLIZING HER POSITION IN RELATION TO MAN.

The Bible attaches deep symbolical meaning to the length of a woman's hair. In Bible days, for a woman to have her hair shaved close and short was a shame and reproach to her. (See 1 Cor. 11:6.) Aside from losing her womanly beauty, she also lost her badge of honor; for her long hair, like the head veil, was considered a symbol of her feminine virtue and propriety.

A woman of honor discreetly covered her head with a veil in public as a mark of her modesty and as an acknowledgment of her God-given position in relation to man. Rebekah, we're told, took a veil and covered herself when she first met Isaac who was to become her husband. The bride of today still wears the traditional head veil when she comes before her groom at the wedding altar.

(A student may read 1 Cor. 11:15.)

"But if a woman have long hair, it is a glory to her: for her hair is given her for a covering."

Long hair is a woman's head covering.

Here the apostle Paul calls a woman's long hair her "glory" because it serves as a "head covering." In other words, a woman's long hair provides a "natural veil" for her head; and therefore like the head veil, signifies modesty, honor and virtue, as well as submission to her God-appointed place in life.

(A student may read 1 Tim. 2:12, 13, and 1 Cor. 11:3.)

"But I suffer not a woman . . . to usurp authority over the man . . . for Adam was first formed, then Eve."

"The head of every man is Christ; and the head of the woman is the man."

A woman's long hair mysteriously and symbolically denotes her acceptance of man's authority over her.

5. THE TWO SEXES — THOUGH DIFFERENT — COMPLEMENT EACH OTHER. BOTH ARE EQUAL BEFORE GOD.

Is man superior to woman? Has God pitted one against the other? **Not at all!** Instead, each **needs** the other, and each **complements** the other!

Woman is the counterpart of the man.

Just as the clay is the counterpart of the clay mold, so is the woman the counterpart of the man. Though the shape of the clay and the shape of the mold are similar — yet one is the exact opposite of the other! Where one is concave, the other is convex.

Can we say that the clay is more important than the mold? Or that the mold is more important than the clay? No, for **only as the two are combined can each perfectly demonstrate its own unique value!**

Men and women are equally important.

Man is incomplete without the woman, and woman is incomplete without the man. A woman therefore has an equal right to take pride in her femininity as does a man to take pride in his masculinity. Each is equally important to the other. The apostle Paul gives us a beautiful expression of this relationship in his first letter to the Corinthians.

(A student may read 1 Cor. 11:11, 12.)

"Nevertheless neither is the man without the woman, neither the woman without the man, in the Lord. For as the woman is of the man, even so is the man also by the woman; but all things of God."

Both are equal before God.

Though the wife is called the "weaker vessel," yet she stands equal to her husband before the Lord.

(A student may read 1 Peter 3:7.)

"Likewise, ye husbands, dwell with them according to knowledge, giving honour unto the wife, as unto the weaker vessel, and as being heirs together of the grace of life."

God has ordained a beautiful relationship between the sexes where each needs the other and both need God!

Prayer:

Lord, help us to realize the part our sexuality plays in your plan for our lives. Help us to maintain our sexual uniqueness so that we may complement one another. May we be proud to look like men, and may we be "real men" through Jesus Christ, our Lord. Amen.

Memory Question No. 6: Are we acting in accordance with God's purposes when we blur the distinction between male and female?

Answer: "So God created man in his own image, in the image of God created he him; male and female created he them" (Gen. 1:27).

EATING FOR PHYSICAL FITNESS

(Pages 42 — 49, Student's Training Manual)

PRIOR TO CLASS: Cut out parts for "Successful Sam" Skit from pages 217 and 219. Select 3 boys to perform in skit.

YOU WILL NEED: Bathroom-type floor scales. Table, chair, balloon and potato chip box (for the skit).

WHY IS PHYSICAL FITNESS IMPORTANT?

Why should God's man keep physically fit? Does he have a greater reason to take good care of his body than someone who cares nothing about pleasing God or obeying him?

Let your students give their ideas about this. Then continue as follows:

1. The body is God's property.

God's man should keep physically fit because he is "not his own" but has been "bought with a price." (See 1 Cor. 6:19, 20.) His body belongs to God — **not to himself!** To treat **God's property** with disrespect is equivalent to treating **God** with disrespect! To illustrate this truth, consider the case of Dick and his dog:

> When Dick left town to go on vacation with his family, his friend Morris agreed to take care of his dog. Dick was confident that his dog would receive good treatment.
>
> Returning home he found his once sleek and bright-eyed pet turned into a sad-looking creature with bedraggled hair and dull eyes. What had happened?
>
> Morris, instead of exercising the dog regularly, had kept him cooped up in a small pen. Instead of providing fresh water and shade, Morris often left the animal exposed to the hot sun with nothing more than a few drops of water to drink. Although Dick had provided him with a generous supply of dog food, Morris failed to feed the animal regularly.

Who did Morris "sin against" in this situation? The dog? The dog's owner? Or both?

Let the students give their ideas.

By failing to provide adequate care, Morris abused the animal, to be sure. But in knowingly abusing Dick's property, Morris also sinned against Dick, the owner of the property! The same is true when we knowingly abuse our bodies. We not only sin against our bodies but also against the one to whom they belong — our Creator God!

2. Physical energy is necessary to work for God.

God's man should keep physically fit in order for him to be sure of a good supply of vitality. The fellow who is determined to accomplish things for Jesus Christ will need strength and energy for the job. Jesus' band of disciples in the 1st century could not afford to be "softies." Neither can we in this 20th century!

3. Spiritual vitality must be preserved.

God's man will want to keep physically fit so that he will not drain his spiritual vitality! What does one's physical condition have to do with his spiritual vitality? Man is composed of more than flesh and bones; a spirit lives within his body, too. Man's spirit and body are not independent of each other. One affects the other. Although a man may possess a sturdy spirit within a weak body, normally sturdy spirits are found in sturdy bodies. For man's spirit and body are mysteriously inter-related.

THE SPIRITUAL AFFECTS THE PHYSICAL

In the first cartoon strip (page 42, Training Manuals) we read: When a man breaks a spiritual law (by telling a lie, for instance) . . . not only his spirit is affected, but also his body. (That's why the lie detector works.)

God's Word says, "Be sure your sin will find you out" (Num. 32:23). And sin does "find you out" in your body! According to the medical profession, continued sins of the spirit such as anger, fear, hate and resentment can cause ulcers, high blood pressure, stomach disorders and other ailments. Dr. George Comstock of John Hopkins University conducted tests which show that men who attend church regularly stand twice the chance of avoiding fatal heart attacks, cancer, tuberculosis, chronic bronchitis, and cirrhosis of the liver. Medical science acknowledges that a man's spiritual condition affects his body.

THE PHYSICAL AFFECTS THE SPIRITUAL

A man's physical condition likewise can affect his spirit. Look at the second cartoon strip. Here we read: When a man breaks a law of health, not only his body is affected, but also his spirit! Since we have no mechanical instrument capable of measuring "spiritual vitality," we cannot prove this principle scientifically. But we know it to be true not only on the basis of God's Word, but also by human logic and experience.

TO HARM THE BODY IS SIN

Have your students read 1 Cor. 6:19 and 1 Cor. 3:16, 17.

"What? know ye not that your body is the temple of the Holy Ghost which is in you, which ye have of God, and ye are not your own" (1 Cor. 6:19)?

"Know ye not that ye are the temple of God, and that the Spirit of God dwelleth in you? If any man defile the temple of God, him shall God destroy; for the temple of God is holy, which temple ye are" (1 Cor. 3:16, 17).

SIN AGAINST THE BODY LOWERS SPIRITUAL VITALITY

As we have already pointed out, when we needlessly harm our bodies, we are sinning against God's property. What does sin do to our spiritual condition?

Every sin we commit (no matter how small) weakens our spiritual condition and saps our spiritual vitality!

For instance, when we gobble 3 chocolate bars in a row, or "party" until early morning, or lounge all weekend watching T.V. (instead of getting fresh air and exercise), we suffer a proportionate "leakage" of spiritual power.

The glutton's interest in food dulls his interest in God! The lounge-lizard's love of ease lessens his zest for God's work! The chain smoker, drunkard or drug addict who surrenders his human "will" to these habits soon finds he has no "will" left to serve God!

DISCIPLINE KEEPS THE BODY IN SUBJECTION

Since "no man can serve two masters" (see Matt. 6:24), every fellow faces this question: **Who will be the master or "boss" of my life? Will I be ruled by my bodily desires or by God?**

The apostle Paul made his decision. He said, "I keep under my body and bring it into subjection" (1 Cor. 9:27). Like an athlete in training, Paul maintained rigid discipline over his body. Paul didn't want to be replaced on "God's team." He didn't want to be relegated to the sidelines as a useless cast-off!

But the record shows Paul was no "bench-warmer." Instead he was a star performer who saw plenty of action! The discipline he practiced gave him the grit necessary to carry him through some exciting adventures for God.

PHYSICAL AND SPIRITUAL DISCIPLINE GO TOGETHER

Discipline likewise paid off for those 3 tough-minded teen-agers — Shadrack, Meshach and Abednego. Why didn't their spiritual knees buckle when they faced the fiery furnace? Because they'd already learned the meaning of discipline!

These same young men who refused to corrupt themselves **spiritually** by worshipping the golden image had previously refused to corrupt themselves **physically** by indulging in the king's food and wine. (See Dan. 1:5-15.)

"Coddle the body and you harm the soul." So states an ancient proverb which still holds true today. One of the goals therefore in our Training Program is to develop **the disciplined physical toughness** that goes hand in hand with **disciplined spiritual toughness.**

To keep our bodies in top physical condition demands discipline in two areas: (1) in our eating, and (2) in our exercising. In this training session, we'll concentrate on the first of these two areas.

LET'S "WEIGH IN"!
(Page 43, Student's Training Manual)

Is your weight normal according to your age and height? To find out, let's "measure up" and "weigh in"!

Measure height of each student (without shoes) standing against the wall. (Tape a measuring rule to the wall.) Weigh students on bathroom type floor scales. Have them record their height and weight in their Training Manuals along with their standard weight taken from the weight table provided. If the student's weight is above or below the "average standard weight," he may enter the amount of difference in his chart.

THE SECRET OF MAINTAINING PROPER WEIGHT: BALANCE YOUR "INTAKE" AND "OUTPUT"!
(Page 44, Student's Training Manual)

Your body weight depends upon two things — and each is subject to your control: (1) your "intake" (the calories you consume in the food you eat), and (2) your "output" (the calories you burn in the energy you expend). When your intake **exceeds your output,** you gain weight. When your output **exceeds your intake,** you lose weight. When your intake and output **are equal,** you neither lose nor gain.

Have your students figure the weight problems given on page 44 of their Training Manuals. Note that 3600 calories = 1 lb. Answers are as follows:

8-1/3 pounds gained
5 pounds drained.
No gain or loss.

Generally speaking, weight gain or loss is a matter of simple arithmetic! What's not so simple, however, is to form the right "intake-output" habits so as to maintain your proper weight level.

In a moment we'll eavesdrop on a telephone conversation involving 3 fellows whose "intake-output" habits vary considerably — "Mac the Muncher," "Lazy Larry," and "Successful Sam." As you listen, check to see if you recognize any of your acquaintances — **or perhaps yourself** — in one of the 3 characters.

"SUCCESSFUL SAM" SKIT

Props required are as follows:
A chair placed at front of room near the hall opening.
A small table beside the chair.
A potato chip box placed on the table. (This may be empty, and the potato chip munching may be simulated.)
A pillow or inflated balloon to stuff inside Mac the Muncher's shirt to give him an appearance of being overweight.

As skit is announced, "Successful Sam" takes his position at front of classroom standing at the far side away from the hall opening. Mac the Muncher and Lazy Larry both await entrance in side hall. Mac the Muncher places balloon or pillow inside his shirt to resemble a large, rounded stomach. You, the teacher, may announce the skit as follows:

Teacher: As our skit opens, it's 10 o'clock Saturday morning. Successful Sam is at home making a telephone call. *(Sam makes motions as though dialing.)* Ding-a-ling-aling! The telephone is ringing at the other side of town at the home of two brothers, Mac the Muncher and Lazy Larry. I wonder which one will answer the phone . . . Oh, I see it's Mac the Muncher!

Mack the Muncher enters from side hall, walks slowly toward the table, chewing obviously as he picks up the receiver. (To free his hands, Mac lays his lines on the table in front of him.)
Mac: *(Swallowing hard and licking his lips as he picks up the phone.)* (Gulp!) Hello!
Sam: Hi, Mac! This is Sam! Did I get you from something?
Mac: Naw . . . I was just finishing a jelly doughnut left over from breakfast. What's on your mind? *(Mack picks up potato chip box and smiles with anticipation as he peers into it.)*
Sam: Oh, nothing special! Didn't get to see you at school yesterday. How'd it go for you?
Mac: *(Grabbing a handful of potato chips out of the box and chewing on them noisily.)* Oh . . . (chomp, chomp) . . . pretty boring, I'd say . . . (chomp, chomp) that is, until I stopped at the Ice Cream Shoppe on the way home (chomp, chomp). That hot fudge sundae really hit the spot! (chomp, chomp.)
Sam: What'd you say? I'm having a hard time hearing you. There's some loud crackling in my ear! We must have a bad connection!
Mac: *(Still munching.)* That's funny . . . (chomp, chomp) I can hear you just fine! Let's see now, what have I been doing? Well, I went to Boy's Club last night, but it was sure dull! That is, until they brought out the cupcake and hot chocolate. I woke up fast then! Professor Perkins should have seen me! He complains about me being lethargic and dull in his English class!
Sam: Yea, the Prof is pretty demanding! His tests are sticklers too! That reminds me . . . have you studied for the test he's giving Monday?

Mac: Yeah ... I hit the books when I got home from the Boy's Club meeting. But studying late makes me famished! Had to raid the refrigerator to survive! Boy, Mom makes the best apple pie!

Sam: Say, Mac ... they're holding Junior Varsity try-outs Monday. Are you going to show up?

Mac: Naw! No use, Sam! The coach has it in for me! Says I'm too slow! He's sure unreasonable! Can I help it if I'm just naturally heavy? How about you, Sam? Will you try out?

Sam: Sure thing!

Mac: Well, with your physique, they'll grab you fast! Some guys are born lucky! *(Heaves a big sigh.)* Not me though! *(Droops his shoulders.)* Man, I'm low on energy this morning! I need an early lunch today. I'd better call you back after I've eaten. But wait ... I see my lazy brother's finally crawled out of bed! Wanna talk to him?

Sam: Sure ... put him on! *Larry walks into room, yawning and stretching.*

Mac: *(Handing phone to Lazy Larry.)* Here, Larry ... it's Sam!

Larry: *(Drowzily, still standing.)* Hi, Sam ... how're things?

Sam: Really great, Larry! But where were you yesterday? Missed you in gymn class!

Larry: Oh, I got excused! Told Mr. Harris I was dizzy! Well ... I did feel sort of tired ... and it was a relief to get out of that hurdle-leaping! Who wants to play like a leap-frog anyway!

Sam: Did you get to the game after school?

Larry: Naw ... I borrowed a bus pass and rode downtown to the main library to check out a book I've been wanting to read. My old man thought I should've walked! But he forgets how tired a guy gets sittin' in a stuffy old school building all day! *(Pauses, and looks around.)* Just a minute Sam. I want to take a seat here! *(Sinks into the chair, heaving a big sigh as though exhausted.)* Guess I got out of bed too early this morning. I'm one of those guys that requires lots of rest!

Sam: Sure, Larry! Are you O.K. now?

Larry: Yeah ... I think so. Now, where were we? Oh, yeah ... the library. Well, I got a science fiction book, and spent the rest of the day in bed reading! It was really neat! But what's new with you, Sam?

Sam: Well ... for one thing, I'm going swimming this afternoon! How about coming along?

Larry: *(Shaking his head firmly.)* No, siree! Not me! Today's my only day to rest! And besides, I want to finish this book to see if the space man captures the Mars monster or not.

Sam: But I'll see you at the Youth Skate tonight, won't I?

Larry: Naw ... not much reason for me to go. The girls don't skate with me anyway! They all cluster around you, Sam! Wonder what makes them so unfriendly! *(Stretching.)* Ho ... hum! Just talking about skating makes me tired all over! Maybe if I get comfortable here, I'll feel better. *(Sprawling out on floor, and propping his feet up on a chair.)* Yeah ... this is more like it! *(Sighs pleasantly.)* Now, Sam, I want to hear how your day went yesterday. I'll just rest here while you talk.

Sam: Well, Larry, I really had a red letter day! Awoke feeling great . . . got off to my usual good start . . . and the whole day just fell in place — like that!

Larry: Hold on here a minute . . . what do yah mean —your "usual good start?" You got a secret formula or something?

Sam: Oh, no . . . not anything special . . . really . . . I just kick back the covers every morning . . . jump out of bed and do some deep-breathing exercises before I get dressed. Then I read my Bible, eat breakfast and go off to school feeling like a winner!

Larry: Ugh! Sounds awful to me! Too much exertion so early in the morning! But speaking of winners . . . who won the game yesterday after school?

Sam: We did! Trimmed Stanley High 81 to 60! Somehow I managed to make 14 baskets! Everyone gathered around to talk afterward, and I missed my bus home. Didn't mind the walk though.

Larry: Did you stop at the Ice Cream Shoppe?

Sam: Nope! I'm in training! And besides, I wanted to be able to enjoy a good square meal when I got home! So I just ate the apple I'd saved from lunch. Ran into Betty though, and we had a real good time talking all the way home!

Larry: Are you taking her to the Youth Skate tonight?

Sam: No, but she asked if I'd be there . . . and she looked real happy when I said I would. She said she'd be seeing me! Come to think of it . . . I sure did have a good day!

Larry: Glad someone did! *(Yawn . . .)* Guess I'd better hang up now. This phone is getting . . . awfully . . . heavy . . . *(Drops head on his chest, letting receiver drop.)*

Sam: *(Listening for a moment.)* Larry? Larry?

Larry: *(Making loud snoring noise.)* Zzzz . . . Zzzz . . . Zzzz . . .

Sam: *(Shaking head and hanging up phone.)* Hmm . . . It's easy to see that Mac the Muncher and Lazy Larry are both trapped on the wrong merry-go-round! They should read page 45 in the Training Manual!

END OF SKIT

HOW TO CONTROL THE "MERRY-GO-ROUNDS"
(Page 45, Student's Training Manual)

Have your students read the paragraphs entitled "Merry-Go-Round No. 1" and "Merry-Go-Round No. 2" at the top of page 45 in their Training Manuals. (Merry-go-round "wheels" are pictured below each paragraph.)

Successful Sam was right. "Mac the Muncher" and "Lazy Larry" were last seen riding Merry-Go-Round No. 1. It's not surprising that they're both on the same merry-go-round, because actually "Mac the Muncher" and "Lazy Larry" are often linked together like Siamese twins!

The extra weight caused by Mac's in-between-meal nibbling makes him so tired that he shuns exercise (like Lazy Larry) which in turn adds more fat . . . which makes him even more lethargic . . . **and around and around he goes!**

Likewise, the inactive fellow (like Lazy Larry) who shuns exercise and youth activities, becomes so bored with life that he nibbles (like Mac the Muncher), which adds more weight, which in turn makes him even more inactive — **and around and around he goes!**

They're both trapped on the wrong merry-go-round! Will they ride forever? They don't have to! There's a way to stop the merry-go-round to allow them to get off! But before we look into the "secret control lever" that controls both of these merry-go-rounds (No. 1 and No. 2), let's consider the various sections of the two merry-go-round wheels pictured in our Training Manuals.

CAN YOU IDENTIFY THE MERRY-GO-ROUND SECTIONS?

Have your students enter the missing words on the dotted lines following the directions given in their Training Manuals.

When correctly completed, Merry-Go-Round No. 1 is made up of: "BETWEEN-MEAL NIBBLING" which causes "EXTRA WEIGHT" which produces "LETHARGY" which encourages "INACTIVITY" which leads to "BOREDOM" (which leads to) "BETWEEN-MEAL-NIBBLING."

Merry-Go-Round No. 2 is made up of: "A CORRECT DIET" which produces "VITALITY" which encourages "REGULAR EXERCISE" which increases "MENTAL VIGOR" which helps maintain "A DISCIPLINED LIFE" (which leads to) "A CORRECT DIET."

MERRY-GO-ROUND CONTROL BOX

Read Item No. 1 of the Operating Instructions. Have your students de-code the "Secret Control Lever" at the bottom of page 45 in their Training Manuals. "D-I-S-C-I-P-L-I-N-E" is the message on the "Secret Control Lever."

Read Item No. 2 of the Operating Instructions. Call attention to the note at the bottom of the page. Explain that "discipline" is the secret control that will allow a fellow to stop "BETWEEN-MEAL NIBBLING" (Merry-Go-Round No. 1) and that "discipline" is also the secret control that will enable him to start "A CORRECT DIET" (Merry-Go-Round No. 2). Emphasize that discipline is required for both operations!

CALORIE CHART
(Page 46, Student's Training Manual)

How many calories should you consume each day? If you are between 13 and 15 years of age, your average daily requirement is approximately 3100 calories. If you're more than 15 years of age, it is approximately 3600 calories.

This figure varies with the amount of energy you burn. When you're climbing a mountain, for example, you can use more calories without adding weight than when you're putting a model plane together. As we have learned from page 44 of our Training Manuals, our daily "intake" of food should balance with our daily "output" of energy.

Don't be fooled by the innocent appearance of those in-between-meal snacks. They can be loaded! Let's count the extra calories Mac munched in less than a 24-hour period.

Write the following food items on the chalkboard. Have your students give you the calorie count of each item from the Calorie Chart in their Training Manuals.

Jelly Doughnut (left over from breakfast) ....(225) calories
Potato chips (while talking on phone) ....(110) calories
Fudge sundae (on way home from school)......(465) calories
Cupcake (at Boy's Club meeting)....................(145) calories
Hot chocolate (at Boy's Club meeting)............(200) calories
Apple pie (when studying late) ....(345) calories
Total "Between-Meal-Munching"..................(1,490) calories

If Mac's daily calorie requirement were 3100 (the normal amount for a 13 to 15-year old boy), he munched approximately 48% of his daily requirement without eating even one meal! He might have tried these low-calorie snacks instead:

Write these food items on the chalkboard. Have your students supply the calorie count for each item from their Training Manuals.

Raw carrot...(20) calories
Large stalk of raw celery.....................................(5) calories
Half grapefruit ....(50) calories

Orange...(60) calories
Raw apple...(70) calories
205 calories
or about 6½% of
a 3100 daily
requirement.

Why not get acquainted with the Calorie Chart in your Training Manual? Becoming calorie-conscious will help keep you fit!

"CALORIE GUESSING GAME" *(Optional)*

To help your students become more familiar with the variation in calorie count between various food items, have a "calorie guessing game." Tell the students to close their Training Manuals; then as you call out the names of various food items which appear on the Calorie Chart, challenge them to guess the calorie count of each item. After several have offered their guesses, reveal the correct calorie count.

ARE YOU UNDERWEIGHT?

Even if you're underweight, you'll still need to become calorie-conscious! Here's the way to add pounds: Instead of filling your stomach with bulky low-calorie foods, choose nourishing, high-calorie foods. If you fill up quickly at meal times, increase your total food intake by eating between meals. Snack on items such as peanut butter, cheese, bananas and cream. Try to get at least 8 hours sleep each night. (Nine or 10 would be even better!) But don't overlook outdoor activity either. Fresh air and relaxing recreation are essential to every fellow!

BASIC DAILY DIET

Are you getting your basic daily food requirements?

Refer students to the list of "Basic Daily Requirements" at bottom of page 46 in their Training Manuals. Have your students compare their actual diet in the last 24-hour period with the basic daily requirements listed here, scoring themselves as shown.

If you're serious about achieving a fully-developed manly appearance, be sure to get your share of these body-building basic foods. They're a growing boy's best friend!

You can skip them, of course, and fill up on soft drinks and candy instead; but if you do, be prepared for a pimply complexion, sallow skin, mottled teeth, flabby tissue and a generally under-developed physique. One thing is certain: You cannot avoid the "tell-tale transparency" of your body! Remember this principle: What goes **inside** sooner or later shows up on the **outside**!

WHAT DO YOU FEED YOUR MIND THROUGH YOUR EYES AND EARS?
(Page 47, Student's Training Manual)

Does it matter what you feed your mind? This same principle just mentioned also holds true in regard to what you feed your mind. What you allow inside shows up on the outside, too! The thoughts you "feed on" become your personality, your actions and your habits! **You are what you "think" just as surely as you are what you "eat"!**

Would you eat out of a garbage can? Of course not! You know garbage is unfit for human consumption. Take a look at the 3 garbage cans pictured in your Training Manuals. Read the warnings:

Danger! Rotten, unclean!
Danger! Contaminated with impurities!
Danger! A breeding place for destructive germs!

If ever you are tempted to let your mind "feed on garbage," ask yourself the questions listed on page 47 of your Training Manuals.

(Have your students read these questions aloud, looking up the scripture references given.)

BEWARE OF THE "CURIOSITY TRAP"!

Don't let curiosity tempt you to linger over obscene literature which may fall into your hands. To be overly inquisitive concerning evil, places you in the way of temptation. Beware of this "curiosity trap"! Remember, it caught Adam and Eve. Their inordinate desire to have their eyes opened to "evil" as well as to "good" prompted them to disobey God.

LEARN ABOUT GOOD — NOT EVIL

Of course, it's human to want to know everything there is to know. But why not follow the apostle Paul's advice instead and become knowledgeable about the good things in life rather than the evil? He wrote, "I would have you wise unto that which is good, and simple concerning evil" (Rom. 16:19). "For it is a shame," God's Word says, "even to speak of those things which are done of them in secret" (Eph. 5:12).

God isn't trying to deny us anything good! He's simply trying to protect us from any contamination which might harm us. When you feel the urge to pry into these practices, be good to yourself — squelch it!

GET RID OF POLLUTING MATERIAL

In the book of Acts we're told that many of the new believers brought their evil books together and "burned them before all men" (Acts 19:19). If you've hidden away some books you'd be ashamed for your parents to see — follow the example of these new believers and burn them!

If you receive any pornographic material through the mail (and many pornographic publishers do prey upon teenagers in this way), go immediately to your post office and request a form to fill out, which will restrict the future delivery of such material to you at your home address.

A SENSIBLE PRECAUTION

David gives us a good rule to follow. He wrote, "I will set no wicked thing before mine eyes" (Ps. 101:3). This precaution, though written centuries ago, makes excellent sense today; for science is now aware of the deep-seated effect of the things we set before our eyes. Once an image is deposited upon the sensitive photographic plate of our minds, it is never completely erased. Impure impressions entering the "eyegate " engrave themselves upon a person's thought-life to destroy its wholesomeness and leave in its place a feeling of defilement and guilt.

WHAT DO YOU LISTEN TO?

Your mind is fed though your "eargate" as well as your "eyegate." Don't underestimate the power of the words you listen to! Marxists are not the only ones who know the effectiveness of brainwashing. Satan also is well aware of the suggestive power of a repeated message. That's why he pours forth his propaganda repeatedly from radios, record players and television sets.

WHY GIVE AN EAR TO SATAN'S LIES?

What's the danger in "just listening"? The danger is that Satan's sounds may create such mental "static" in your ears that you cannot distinguish God's voice when he speaks to you!

(Refer students to cartoon at bottom of page 47 in their Training Manuals.)

Without specialized training, prisoners of war who are subjected to sustained brainwashing eventually become unable to distinguish truth from untruth. This can happen to a teenager too. After listening repeatedly to song lyrics depicting drugs and illicit sex as normal and good, a fellow's concept of right and wrong can gradually become blurred. Finally, with God's voice jammed out, he may accept Satan's lie as the truth.

YOU ARE NO PURER THAN YOUR THOUGHTS

To keep yourself pure, keep your thoughts pure! Christ tells us that to dwell purposely on unclean and lustful thoughts is a sin. "Whosoever looketh on a woman to lust after her hath committed adultery with her already in his heart" (Matt. 5:28).

What does the Bible mean by the word "heart"? Proverbs 23:7 gives us a clue. "As he thinketh in his heart, so is he." The "heart" therefore is where we do our "thinking" — the seat of our inner thought-life.

The "heart" is closely tied with our imagination also; for in Genesis 6:5 we read that "every **imagination of the thoughts of his (man's) heart** was only evil continually."

ACTIONS PROCEED FROM THOUGHTS

"But," you may ask "what's wrong with just **thinking** things or **picturing things in your mind** if you'd never actually do them?" God gives us the answer in Proverbs 4:23.

(Have the class read this verse from their Bibles.)

"Keep thy heart with all diligence; for **out of it** are the issues of life." The "issues" of your life (your every action and deed) **proceed from your thoughts and imaginings.** The quality and direction of your thoughts determine the quality and direction of your life! Noble thoughts? A noble life! Low thoughts? A low life! Pure thoughts? A pure life!

THOUGHTS ARE DYNAMITE!

Indulging in mental fantasies is no idle sport. Your thoughts and your imagination generate actions. Your mind, in some peculiar way, tends to provoke (and thus bring about) the very set of peculiar circumstances which allow your thoughts to take shape — to be "acted out." Every impure act began as an impure thought — **perhaps months or years before!** "Keep thy heart with all diligence; for out of it are the issues of life."

BUT HOW DO YOU "KEEP" YOUR HEART?

You "keep" your heart (1) by guarding the material you allow your mind to feed upon; (2) by avoiding anything that would provoke ungodly thoughts or pictures in your mind; (3) by allowing the Holy Spirit to free your mind from unavoidable temptations to look and lust; and (4) by filling your mind with wholesome thoughts — God's kind of thoughts.

Don't feel that you are alone in the battle to keep your thoughts pure. Most teenage boys need help with this problem.

TAKE THE CASE OF 14-YEAR OLD JOE . . .

Joe has just trusted Christ as his Saviour, and he's trying hard to "keep his heart" as the Bible says. He's stopped going to the wrong kind of movies. He's choosing his reading material carefully. He's avoiding any television programs that might encourage impure thoughts.

Joe has found that these precautions do help him maintain a wholesome thought-life. "But even so," he says, "there are some things I just can't avoid! Even though I'm not looking for them, they're just there — all sorts of sights and sounds that bring lustful sex thoughts into my mind. And the more I try to force them out, the stronger they become! What's a fellow to do anyway?"

What is Joe to do?

Is there a way to overcome this problem? **Absolutely!** God hasn't left Joe without help — **or you!** "There hath no temptation taken you but such as is common to man: but God is faithful, who will not suffer you to be tempted above that ye are able; but will with the temptation also make a way to escape, that ye may be able to bear it" (1 Cor. 10:13).

A way of escape is available for Joe — just like the Bible says!

To help us understand how this way of escape operates, let's consider how Joe's mind works. Joe's mind — and yours and mine — are like computers. Every impression we receive through our sense organs is fed into complex storage compartments in our "computer-brains." These impressions may be recalled at will from our "memory-banks," but they may also pop into our conscious minds uninvited. The vividness of the memory and the ease with which they come into our minds depend upon the strength of their "imprint."

Struggling and straining defeats Joe's purpose!

When Joe strains to force an unwanted impression out of his mind, he is actually **increasing** the strength of the imprint in his "memory bank" and thus defeating his own purpose! **Does he need to struggle like that?** No! God has provided **a better way!**

Joe possesses an "automatic rejector unit"!

Ever since Joe trusted Christ as his Saviour, he's been in possession of some highly sensitive equipment which works in conjunction with his "computer-brain." You might call it an "automatic rejector unit." Its purpose? To reject unbidden, ungodly impressions! Its power source? The Holy Spirit!

Joe's "rejector unit" warns him of trouble.

This is how the "automatic rejector" works: Let's say, for example, that Joe flips through the pages of a magazine and is suddenly confronted with a full-page picture of a scantily clad female advertising bath soap! What happens now?

Instantly Joe's spirit-powered "automatic rejector unit" sends a strong **"reject signal"** to his "computer-brain." **"Bzzz . . . zzz . . . zzz!"** Joe's intake system starts flashing trouble-lights! It warns:

"DON'T-FEED-ON-THIS-MATERIAL!
IT-CAN-PRODUCE-LUST!"

Joe is faced with two alternatives.

At this point Joe can either submit his will to God, thus allowing the spirit-empowered "Rejector" full control, or he can resist God's spirit and in so doing cripple the entire system! For one second, Joe is frozen with indecision! Then . . . he makes his choice! **Joe submits himself to God!**

The battle is won!

In that moment **the most potent counteracting force in the world** goes to work for Joe! With mighty power, **the Holy Spirit expels that seducing impression from Joe's conscious mind!** Instantly Joe senses relaxation . . . and peace. No longer is he held in the grip of temptation. **Joe is released!**

With his "computer-brain" now at liberty to receive new impressions, Joe's eyes pass freely beyond the tempting picture to the next page where his attention is drawn to an article on deep-sea fishing. **Joe is safe! He is free!**

What did Joe have to do? Nothing!

Did Joe have to **force** the impression out? **Agonize** over it? **Review it again and again?** No! All Joe had to do was to say, "I'm yours, Lord . . . you take over!" What kind of "recall-imprint" did the picture leave on Joe's brain? Only the weakest imprint with minimal "recall" potential!

But notice carefully the two phases of this operation: (1) expelling the objectionable material from Joe's mind, and (2) welcoming new and acceptable material into Joe's mind.

You may ask, "What if Joe hadn't found an interesting article on the next page? What if there were nothing good to fill his mind with?"

No problem! The Bible gives the answer. "Thy word have I hid in mine heart that I might not sin against thee." If Joe had learned even one verse of scripture "by heart," he could have grabbed that verse out of his memory storehouse. Or he could have simply "zeroed in" on God for a moment, filling his mind with God's thoughts!

But in order to do this, he must be familiar with God's thoughts. Where are God's thoughts found? In the Bible!

Refer your students to page 48, Student's Training Manuals. Call attention to illustration of the boy reading his Bible. Have the students read the scripture verses encircling this boy. Ask your students:

1. What kind of "mind food" is this fellow "feeding upon"?

2. What are some of the wholesome morsels he is "digesting" for later use?

3. Will reading these verses really make a difference in his life?

To help your students give a positive answer to this last question, have them quietly read "Five Promises Concerning God's Word" and "Results You Can Expect in Your Life (If You Feed on the Word With a Sincere, Open Mind)."

Challenge your students to establish a devotional period each day, following the suggestions offered in "Tips to Help You," Page 49, Student's Training Manual.

Encourage them to make use of the "Bible Reading Chart," checking off each chapter when read. Tell them that if they faithfully follow this system, they will complete the reading of the entire New Testament in only 39 weeks.

Prayer:

Father, thank you for our bodies! Help us to eat properly so as to keep them well-nourished and strong. Help us not forget that our "inner man" needs nourishment as well! May we choose wholesome food for our minds and spirits, refusing the "garbage" of this world, so that we may be not only physically fit but also spiritually fit for the service of your Son, Jesus Christ! Amen.

Memory Question No. 7: To enjoy real life, what do we require besides food for our bodies?

Answer: "Man shall not live by bread alone, but by every word that proceedeth out of the mouth of God" (Matt. 4:4).

EXERCISING FOR PHYSICAL FITNESS
(Pages 50 — 53, Student's Training Manual)

PRIOR TO CLASS: Determine whether or not you will invite a school physical education teacher to be "guest-expert" at this session to direct the students in the various calisthenics suggested. Or you yourself may easily guide your students through the Daily "Half-Dozen" exercises illustrated in their Training Manuals as well as the supplementary ones described in your Teacher's Book.

If you plan to have a jogging-running activity (see page 118), provide paper cups and some type of refreshing drink following this, if possible.

DO YOU WANT TO BUILD A BETTER WORLD?

If you want to build a better world, you can start right now by building a better "you"!

When God created Adam, he gave him a perfect body and commanded him to make use of it. He gave Adam a specific job which required him to flex his muscles, stir up his blood and breathe deeply of that purest of all air!

What was this job? God told Adam to cultivate the soil and tend the garden that was to give him food. God's first provisions for Adam, therefore, were twofold: Food and exercise. **If Adam needed both, so do we!**

In our previous training session we learned how to eat properly to keep physically fit. In this session we'll learn how to exercise properly to keep physically fit.

GOD IS IN THE BUSINESS OF BUILDING MEN

A Marine Corps recruiting poster proudly boasts: "The Marine Corps builds men!" To build men the Marine Corps places each recruit under strict discipline in a program of rigorous physical training.

God is also in the business of building men. His program likewise involves discipline and training. To be sure, God wants you to have a sturdy mind and a sturdy spirit — but that's not all. He wants you to have a sturdy body as well. For if you are going to help "shape up the world," **you'll have to be in good shape, too!**

MUSCLES ARE MADE FOR USE!

Start now to follow a program that will keep you in good shape. Become a man of action! God designed your body for motion. That's why he has provided you with more than 600 muscles in your body, including 6 billion amazingly strong muscle fibers, each one capable of supporting 1000 times its own weight. **Are you making good use of these muscles?**

HOW ACTIVE ARE YOU?
(Page 50, Student's Training Manual)

How many hours do you spend each day just sitting, and how many in physical activity?

To help you discover an approximate answer to this question, clock your periods of inactivity as well as your periods of activity throughout a normal day, and record your findings in the charts provided in your Training Manuals (page 50). The results may surprise you!

ARE CORRECTIVE MEASURES NEEDED?

If you discover you're making too little use of the muscles God gave you, formulate a plan of action to remedy the situation. Figure out ways to **decrease** the hours of inactivity which you've recorded on the left side of your chart, by **increasing** the hours of activity which you've recorded on the right side of your chart.

For instance: If you discover that you're spending two or three hours daily in various forms of inactive recreation (watching T.V., talking on the phone with friends, etc.), transfer at least one hour of this into some form of active recreation such as ping-pong, swimming or bicycling. In this way you'll be decreasing your "total time spent sitting" and increasing your "total time spent in action" at the same time.

Of course, many of the "inactivity items" listed in the left column cannot be changed. You can't eat your meals while bicycling, nor can you jog around the classroom! But it is possible to make some changes to allow for more activity in your day. Examine the list. Which items could you change?

Let the students offer ideas. Make the following suggestions:

"INACTIVITY" ITEM NO. 2 — SITTING IN BUS ON WAY TO SCHOOL

Why not set your alarm clock to ring earlier so you'll have time to walk to school? As a precaution against being late, take a "dry run" on a day that school is not in session. Time yourself at a workable speed, then allow for some variation because of traffic or weather conditions.

"INACTIVITY" ITEM NO. 6 — SITTING IN BUS ON WAY HOME FROM SCHOOL

Do you walk into your house feeling exhausted at the end of your school day? If you'll forego the bus ride and walk home instead, your fatigue may vanish. Doctors agree that most fatigue is not physical but mental or emotional, brought on by the stresses and strains of the day. The best way to relieve this kind of nervous fatigue is to engage in some kind of pleasant, moderate exercise. This is nature's way of relaxing muscles and relieving tension after a hard day.

"INACTIVITY" ITEM NO. 10 — SITTING AT TELEPHONE TALKING WITH FRIENDS

This is a common teenager's disease. **Watch out for it!** "Telephonitis" can become crippling! A certain amount of telephone contact with friends is normal and good, but like anything else it can become habit-forming.

"INACTIVITY" ITEM NO. 11 — SITTING IN FRONT OF THE T.V.

Statistics show that this is the greatest time-waster of all! Some guys use T.V. as an escape from life. It becomes an easy way to pass time when they're too lazy to figure out something else to do! **Why let broadcasters steal away your life?** Switch off the "sales-tube" and take an envigorating run around the block, or get started at some productive, creative activity instead! **Your life is important! Don't waste it!**

Now, examine the daily activity listing on the right. Are you failing to put your muscles to work as you should? If this is the case, consider various ways to correct the situation.

"ACTIVITY" ITEM NO. 1 — MUSCULAR WORK

Becoming a "man on the move" means more than simply running around in circles. Spinning circles in a cage may satisfy squirrels — but not men! God designed man as a goal-striving organism. The best form of exercise therefore is the kind God gave Adam to do — **the kind that accomplishes something!** (You'll notice that God did not tell Adam to do 100 push-ups daily!)

If you avoid work, you lose!

Seek out ways to make meaningful use of your muscles — yes, you might even call it "work"! When you perform hard physical work, you gain in 4 ways:

(1) **You develop physical skill and dexterity.**
(2) **You learn how to handle tools and equipment.**
(3) **You build muscles.**
(4) **You build character.**

The fellow who avoids work is actually avoiding a form of pleasure. The most miserable guy in all the world is the one who has **nothing to do!** He is bored and restless. He feels dissatisfied and purposeless. On the other hand, the fellow who is absorbed in creative, constructive work is a happy guy!

Volunteer work spreads happiness.

The most rewarding work is the work you do voluntarily to help others.

• **Is your neighbor having a garage sale?**
   Offer to help him set up the display tables and to clean

up afterwards.
- **Is the family down the street going on a vacation?**
  Offer to mow the lawn, water the shrubs, or care for the animals while they are gone.
- **Is the family next door moving?**
  Give them a hand. Load boxes. Carry out chairs. Sweep out the vacated rooms.
- **Is there an elderly person in your church who has been ill?**
  Offer to help with the yard work, the window washing, or the garage cleaning.

When you put your muscles to work helping someone in need, you're not only creating health for your body but also health for your mind. You're creating happiness for the one you're helping — **and for yourself as well!**

"ACTIVITY" ITEM NO. 2 — DAILY CALISTHENICS

If circumstances prevent your finding enough "work-exercise" to keep your muscles firm and strong, you'll want to supplement your activities with some form of "artificial work" for your body — such as daily calisthenics. These are fine **if you keep them up!** Most boys cease doing calisthenics after a while because their motivation becomes weak. And you must admit push-ups — simply for the sake of push-ups — can become boring!

One way to reinforce your weak motivation is to view your daily workout as partial payment for a product. Let's say that your favorite sport is tennis. You can purchase a good racket and a good pair of tennis shoes, but no store can sell you a good pair of arms! Therefore, view your daily push-ups as a way of **purchasing** a good pair of arms!

"ACTIVITY" ITEM NO. 3 — WALKING (BRISK)

Some believe walking to be the best physical exercise of all. No special equipment is needed, and you can take part in this activity any time of the year. You'll want to start out at an easy pace, then step up gradually until you're walking briskly.

Swing your arms! Work up a light sweat! For maximum body conditioning you should increase your speed until you're breathing hard. (Of course, you'll not want to undertake any unusual exertion without the approval of your doctor.)

"ACTIVITY" ITEM NO. 4 — JOGGING AND RUNNING

Do you get winded playing ball? Does a pounding heart slow you down on a hike? Do your legs get wobbly when you ski, golf or play tennis? Do you need more stamina on hunting and fishing trips? Then get into the jogging-running habit. It will toughen your legs, condition your heart and lungs, and help you develop the kind of muscle-tone you need to enjoy a vigorous life!

"ACTIVITY" ITEM NO. 5 — BICYCLING

Though most boys view their bikes mainly as a means of transportation, actually a bike is a good piece of body-building equipment. A bicycle trip of 2 to 3 miles daily will improve the heart and lung capacity, pep up circulation and toughen the legs.

"ACTIVITY" ITEM NO. 6 — RECREATIONAL ACTIVITY

Everyone needs some kind of fun and relaxation. Working a jigsaw puzzle or playing chess provides pleasant diversion, but this kind of recreation places little demand upon your muscular system — other than your fingers! On the other hand, swimming, hiking, bowling, golf, skiing, tennis, baseball, ping-pong, etc. all offer recreational fun plus the deep breathing which is good for you!

"ACTIVITY" ITEM NO. 7 — GYMN SESSION AT SCHOOL
"ACTIVITY" ITEM NO. 8 — PARTICIPATION IN SPORTS PROGRAM

Of course, you'll spend time in your physical education class at school learning new gymnastic skills and performing with specialized equipment. This is required. Participation in sports and athletic competitions, however, is largely a matter of choice. If the challenge of a competitive sport is an incentive toward keeping fit, this is good.

The apostle Paul told the Corinthian Christians, "Know ye not that they which run in a race run all, but one receiveth the prize? So run, that ye may obtain. And every man that striveth for the mastery is temperate in all things. Now they do it to obtain a corruptible crown; but we an incorruptible. I therefore so run, not as uncertainly; so fight I, not as one that beateth the air: But I keep under my body and bring it into subjection" (1 Cor. 9:24-27).

The apostle Paul told the Corinthian Christians an athlete puts forth extreme effort just for a chance to win a temporary prize, but the Christian's reward is certain and the prize is permanent.

Discipline plays an important role not only in the life of an athlete, but also in the life of a Christian!

YOUR DAILY "HALF-DOZEN"
(Page 50, Student's Training Manual)

A typical daily "half-dozen" is included in your Training Manuals. You may want to add other exercises to fit your special needs, but these will provide a basic plan to work from. Using this as a minimum daily workout, you'll stretch ... sit up ... bicycle ... push ... twist ... and bend ... to get the kinks out of your bodies and to keep yourselves limber!

ADDITIONAL EXERCISES YOU MAY WISH TO PRACTICE

For abdominal muscles:

- Lie on back, hands behind head. Bring yourself up to a sitting position and let yourself down again slowly.

- Lie on floor with your knees straight. Raise feet slowly to count of ten. Lower in same way.

For arms and chest:

- With elbows bent, place palms of hands together at chest level, fingers pointing to chin. Push hard, then release. Repeat 10 times.

- With elbows bent, grip your fingers together at chest level. Pull hard, then release. Repeat 10 times.

For circulation:

- Stand erect with feet together. Swing arms out to the sides and overhead, clapping hands together and at the same time jumping so that feet are spread sideways. Return hands to sides, at the same time jumping so that feet are again together.

WHAT IS YOUR WALKING SPEED?
(Page 51, Student's Training Manual)

When practicing brisk walking, don't meander aimlessly. You'll never know how far you've traveled, or how fast your pace. Instead follow the suggestions given in your Training Manuals for establishing a definite route and determining your walking speed.

Familiarize your students with the "Clocked Time" chart on page 51 of the Student's Training Manual.

Keep a walking chart for a 12-week period. Throughout each week, practice brisk walking whenever and wherever possible. At the end of each week, for clocking purposes, retrace an identical test route so as to provide an accurate speed comparison.

Refer students to Progress Chart in Training Manuals. Read the precautionary note beneath the chart.

JOGGING AND RUNNING TIPS

Have your students read the 5 tips given in their Training Manuals. Have the students practice assuming the correct body position for jogging.

You may want to give your class the opportunity to engage in a group jogging-running activity at the close of this session. Your students would enjoy this. Is there a gymnasium available or a park or field nearby? Provide cold fruit juice or other refreshing drink at the end of this activity, if possible.

PERSONAL "JOG-RUN" PROGRESSION CHART
(Page 52, Student's Training Manual)

Jogging and running benefits do not accrue overnight. They come **gradually,** as you **gradually** intersperse walking with interval jogging and running — and as you **gradually** increase the pace and **gradually** increase the distance traveled.

Remember . . .   gradual progression   is the key to any good jogging-running program!

To record your personal rate of progression, make use of the chart provided on page 52 of your Training Manuals. **Remember that you are not charting your performance so as to measure it against the performance of another fellow. This is your personal, individual record!** Performances vary greatly according to age, weight, muscular development and other inherent factors.

Read the instructions and explain the use of the chart to your class. Emphasize the reason for the "Exercise Score."

Explain that anyone can run-jog-walk at a good pace for a short distance, but to maintain that speed for a longer distance reveals a higher level of achievement. Also, whereas anyone can run-jog-walk for a longer distance if he takes it at a snail's pace, a higher level of achievement is required to go a longer distance while traveling at a faster pace.

Both factors — rate of speed and distance traveled — must be taken into consideration to arrive at a true measure of exercise, or the "Exercise Score."

SPIRITUAL EXERCISE BUILDS SPIRITUAL STRENGTH
(Page 53, Student's Training Manual)

Do you know that a man's spiritual condition can affect his **body strength?** Medical doctors know that fear and guilt can produce actual physical fatigue and muscular weakness. God's Word recorded this phenomenon thousands of years ago when David described these very symptoms when he was carrying the burden of unconfessed sin. He wrote:

"My strength faileth because of mine iniquity" (Ps. 31:10).

"Neither is there any health in my bones because of my sin . . . I am bowed down greatly . . . I am feeble and sore broken . . . My heart panteth, my strength faileth me" (Ps. 38:3, 6, 8, 10).

The Bible says, "Watch ye, stand fast in the faith, quit you like men, be strong" (1 Cor. 16:13). In other words, **act like men! Act like real men . . . strong men!**

HOW CAN YOU BECOME A SPIRITUAL "STRONG MAN"?

To become a spiritual "strong man" you must subject your spirit to training just as you do your body! **Exercise your** soul! Notice the words of Henry Drummond quoted in your Training Manuals at the top of page 53:

"If a man does not exercise his arm, he develops no biceps muscle; and if a man does not exercise his soul, he acquires no muscle in his soul, no strength of character, no vigor of moral fiber, nor beauty of spiritual growth."

WHAT CAN YOU DO TO EXERCISE YOUR SOUL?

The most effective exercise for the soul is the daily exercise of prayer. This is guaranteed to strengthen you! Fail to perform this spiritual exercise regularly, however, and you're sure to become a powerless Christian. It's just as someone said: "Seven prayerless days makes one weak!"

The "spiritual exercise of prayer" practiced daily creates man-sized spiritual muscles. Try it and see!

THE WEAKLING GIVES IN . . . THE STRONG MAN RESISTS!

One word of caution: Be prepared for opposition from the enemy! The moment you decide to pray, an army of foes will swoop down upon you to foil the action! Distractions will enter your mind! Drowziness will overtake you! Hunger pains may demand a trip to the kitchen! You may even decide you should do your homework!

The weakling allows these enemies to overcome him. But in giving in to them, he becomes even weaker for the next battle. The strong man resists and conquers these enemies. And in so doing, he strengthens his muscles for the next battle.

The more you exercise, the easier the going! Stop for a while — and the going gets rough! The more you pray, the easier it is to pray!

"PRAYER-CONTACT" WITH JESUS CHANGES A MAN

The more time you spend in prayer-contact with the Lord, the more your characteristics and personality become like his. Henry Drummond described this phenomenon this way:

"Put a piece of iron in the presence of a magnetized body, and that piece of iron for a time becomes magnetized. It is changed into a temporary magnet in the mere presence of a permanent magnet, and as long as you leave the two side by side, they are both magnets alike. Remain side by side with Him . . . and you, too, will become a permanent magnet . . . and like Him you will draw all men unto you."

PRAYER HELPS DEVELOP A "JESUS-PERSONALITY"

If you want to have a "Jesus-personality" — one that is both manly and magnetic, then spend time in "prayer-contact" with Jesus!

No other personality in all the world attracts men like that of Jesus Christ! The closer you stay to him and the more time you spend talking to him in prayer, the more you will become like him! And as you acquire a personality that reflects Jesus Christ, God will use you to draw others to him.

In this way you'll be doing your part to change the world. For there's only one way to change the world, and that is to change men — **deep inside** where it counts!

The man that is needed by the world today is not the "spiritual softie" but the **"spiritual strong man"** who has developed supernatural strength and power because he has been faithful in exercising his soul in prayer each day!

HOW TO PRAY

Read the 7 tips on "how to pray" which are given in the Student's Training Manual. Encourage your students to start a prayer list.

Teacher, do you transmit a spirit of real enthusiasm as you talk about prayer? Your students will catch this spirit from you! Your enthusiasm will inspire them more quickly than your words. If blessings have come to you through talking to God in prayer, share this with your class. Nothing sells a product more quickly than a satisfied customer!

DO YOU MEASURE UP TO GOD'S CHAMPION?

What is our goal? Colossians 4:12: "That ye may stand perfect and complete in all the will of God." What is the stature we are to strive for? Ephesians 4:13: "Till we all come . . . unto a perfect man, unto the measure of the stature of Christ."

Are you keeping spiritually fit? Are you in perfect form? Do you measure up to "God's champion"? Compare yourself to this description of God's champion. Silently take stock of your spiritual fitness.

COMPARE YOUR MUSCLES!

God's champion has muscles that are exercised daily in prayer. "In the morning will I direct my prayer unto thee, and will look up" (Psalm 5:3).

Ask yourself: Do I stretch my spiritual muscles each morning by beginning my day with prayer, even if brief?

COMPARE YOUR SHOULDERS!

God's champion has shoulders that are broad enough to bear others' burdens. "Bear ye one another's burdens, and so fulfill the law of Christ" (Gal. 6:2).

Ask yourself: When difficulties arise in my home, do I cheerfully do my part to lighten the load?

COMPARE YOUR CHEST!

God's champion has a chest that is not "puffed up." "Love vaunteth not itself, is not puffed up" (1 Cor. 13:4).

Ask yourself: Do I proudly flaunt good grades or other achievements before others?

COMPARE YOUR BACK!

God's champion has a back that is firm with a strong "backbone." "Watch ye, stand fast in the faith . . . be strong" (1 Cor. 16:13).

Ask yourself: Is my backbone strong? Do I stand firm and say "no" when friends urge me to do wrong?

COMPARE YOUR KNEES!

God's champion has knees that are limber, ready to kneel in submission. "Every knee shall bow to me . . . every one of us shall give account of himself to God" (Rom. 14:11,12).

Ask yourself: Do I submit my choice of friends, my amusements, my ambitions to the will of God for my life?

COMPARE YOUR FEET!

God's champion has feet that are sure-footed and confident. "He shall direct thy path . . . thy foot shall not stumble" (Prov. 3:6, 23).

Ask yourself: When I hit a snag or rocky path in my teen years, do I turn to the Lord for direction and help?

COMPARE YOUR ENERGY!

God's champion has energy that is well-preserved . . . not drained by needless anxiety. "Be careful for nothing; but in everything by prayer and supplication with thanksgiving let your requests be made known unto God" (Phil. 4:6).

Ask yourself: Do I preserve my spiritual stamina and vitality by casting off heavy burdens in prayer?

SPIRITUAL FITNESS PAYS DIVIDENDS FOREVER!

God's Word tells us in 1 Tim. 4:8, "Bodily exercise profiteth for a little: but godliness is profitable unto all things, having promise of the life that now is, and of that which is to come."

Physical fitness is vital to our lives on earth here and now; but spiritual fitness is important not only for this present life but also for our eternal lives forever and ever and ever!

Prayer:

Lord, you have given us 600 amazing muscles in our bodies. Help us to exert the discipline necessary to keep them firm and strong. Help us to walk some of the time rather than ride. Help us to work rather than sit. Help us to spend some of our muscle-power helping others rather than doing our own pleasure. May we also exercise our prayer-muscles daily so that we may be strong-hearted men for your Son, Jesus Christ! Amen.

Memory Question No. 8: What results can we expect in our lives when we wait upon God in prayer?

Answer: "They that wait upon the LORD shall renew their strength; they shall mount up with wings as eagles; they shall run, and not be weary; and they shall walk, and not faint. (Isa. 40:31.)

CHOOSING THE RIGHT KIND OF CLOTHES

(Pages 54 — 57, Student's Training Manual)

YOU WILL NEED: One can of food from which the label has been removed and another can of food bearing a false label. See further instructions for this object lesson on page 126.

PRIOR TO CLASS: Determine whether or not you will ask a "guest expert" to assist you during this session. Is there a member of your church who is connected with men's apparel? You may want him to bring samples of "mix and match" outfits or other clothing accessories (belts, socks, etc.) to show the students.

DOES IT MATTER HOW YOU DRESS?

Refer your students to the cartoons of "Phoney-Philip" on page 54 of their Training Manuals. Have your students read the text accompanying the illustrations.

Read aloud the questions listed under "What Is Your Opinion?" Let the students write their answers at this time. (The instruction to follow may modify the viewpoints of some of your students.)

Why should we be concerned about our appearance? Does it make any real difference how we dress? Is **what we are on the inside** the only thing that really matters or is our **outer** appearance important also?

True, the Bible does tell us that whereas man looks at a person's outer appearance, God looks at our hearts. (See 1 Sam. 16:7.) And we all know that how we look to God is the most important thing! Nevertheless (and even as this same scripture acknowledges) man **does** look at our outward appearance! And even as we have an obligation to see that our hearts are clean and pleasing to **God,** we also have an obligation to see that our appearance is clean and pleasing to **man!** *Write the following on the chalkboard:*

We should be concerned with our appearance . . .
1. Because this shows love to our neighbor.
2. Because our appearance becomes our "label."
3. Because people judge us by our clothing.

REASON NO. 1 —
THIS SHOWS LOVE TO OUR NEIGHBOR

The first commandment, Jesus said, is to love God. But the second commandment, which closely follows, is to love our neighbor. If our clothes are grimy or smelly, are we acting in love toward the one who must sit beside us on the bus? If our appearance is repulsive or nauseating, are we acting in love toward the one who must eat beside us at the table?

What it all adds up to is this: If we love God, we'll not want to grieve him with a contemptible, debased heart. And if we love our neighbor, we'll not want to offend him with a contemptible or debased appearance. The Bible says, "Love worketh no ill to his neighbour" (Rom. 13:10). This gives us a good reason to be concerned with our appearance — to show love to our neighbor!

REASON NO. 2 —
OUR APPEARANCE BECOMES OUR "LABEL."

Hold up a can of food from which the label has been removed. Ask the students to tell you what kind of food is inside. After they have made several guesses, tell them what the can contains. (The more unusual the food item, the better.)

Then ask this question: How would you like to shop for groceries in a store where the label has been removed from every can? What does this show us about labels? What conclusions can we draw?

Write on the chalkboard this conclusion:

Labels are important when you can't "see" what's inside!

Now, hold up another can of food which bears a false label which you have prepared beforehand as follows: Prior to class, remove the label from a can of food by slitting it at the back. Choose a can of common size and shape. The food item shown on this label should be one that is not appealing when eaten cold from the can, such as spinach or pumpkin.

Now, affix this "false label" to a second can of the same size and shape but containing a different food item — one which the students might enjoy from the can, such as shoestring potatoes, ripe olives, peanuts, or fruit juice.

Use cellophane tape to close the slit edges at the back of the can. Keep the slit edges out of view so that the students will not suspect that the label is false. Now, ask your students:

"Can you tell me what's inside this can?"

They will answer "Pumpkin " or "Spinach " or whatever the false label reads.

"What makes you think so?"

The students will probably respond, "The label says so! And that's what's pictured on it!"

Then you answer: "Yes, you're right . . . it does say 'pumpkin,' doesn't it! And there's a picture, too! I imagine this is making you mighty hungry for some cold canned pumpkin!

"How many of you just love to eat cold, canned pumpkin? Do you want me to open the can so we can all enjoy some right now?"

(Your students will not be anxious for this "treat." Proceed with the demonstration ignoring any who might playfully insist that they do want some.)

"So, you don't really care for any? It doesn't appeal to you? I really do agree with you! Who wants to eat cold canned pumpkin? Ugh! Sounds **repulsive!** But it would be a shame to throw this can away. So, perhaps I'd better open it anyway!"

Invite your students to gather around as you open the can. When the contents are revealed, express your surprise:

"Well . . . **yummy!** Shoestring potatoes! (Or, "olives" . . . or whatever item you've selected.) That's strange! The label plainly read **'pumpkin'!** I never would have suspected there was anything as good as this inside the can! You'd certainly never guess it from the label, would you?"

Empty the can into a container and invite your students to share the food item. It if is liquid, provide paper cups. Continue as follows:

What does this experience with the false label show us? Does it give us another reason for being concerned with our outward appearance?

Give the students an opportunity to express their thoughts on this.

Should a label "lie"?

Everyone's appearance **"says"** something, just like this label does. Should it give out a false message like this label did?

We live in a world composed of human beings who are not all-knowing. They cannot see what goes on inside our hearts! They must form their ideas about the real person **inside** from the clues furnished on the **outside** (just like we had to do with this canned food). And in their estimation, the way we **dress** is a first-rate clue! It becomes our "label." And for this reason, it is important.

Refer your students again to the statement written on the chalkboard.

LABELS ARE IMPORTANT WHEN YOU CAN'T "SEE" WHAT'S INSIDE!

What happens when a label tells a "lie"?

Consider the case of John Jones. On the inside John was a real "peach" of a fellow. But on the outside we might say he looked something like a "cockroach"! His clothing and hair style labeled him as one of a rebellious gang that was undermining the standards of the community where he lived. Of course, the outer label he wore was a false one. Inside, you recall, John Jones was a real "peach"! But people judged John Jones by his label.

People believe labels and react accordingly.

If a label on a can should plainly read "Stewed Cockroaches" and the picture showed some large, ugly insects, **how would you react?** You'd shy away from that can even though it actually contained luscious, good-tasting peaches! That's exactly what happened to John Jones.

His teachers viewed him with suspicion. His prospective employers turned him away flatly. The nice girls he wanted to date ignored him. His friends became fewer, for their parents refused to let them associate with him.

John finally demanded hotly, "Why can't people treat me like **a decent human being?**"

Someone should have told him: "If you want to be treated like a decent human being, John Jones, you're going to have to **look like one!**"

Remember: Labels are important. And your appearance becomes your label.

REASON NO. 3 —
PEOPLE JUDGE US BY OUR CLOTHING

Call attention to cartoons on page 55, Student's Training Manual. Read aloud and discuss briefly.

"But people have no right to judge a person by his clothes!" you protest.

This may be true. Yet when we look at the history of mankind, we see that clothing has always been used to proclaim a person's state or position in life.

To be clothed in purple, for example, indicated wealth or royalty. For a bride to be attired in white proclaimed her purity. Grief was once expressed by wearing sack cloth. Mourning is expressed by wearing black. The special clothing worn by doctors, firemen, policemen, milk men, mail carriers, bakers, chefs, soldiers and sailors identifies their role in life.

The habit of judging a person by his clothing is deeply ingrained in humanity and cannot easily be shaken.

A changed appearance will produce a changed attitude.

If you want to change people's attitude toward you, you can begin by changing your outward appearance. People do judge you by your appearance.

An attorney on the West Coast had to face up to this fact. To make sure his clients got a fair break, he shaved off his beard. He feared his appearance might subconsciously prejudice the jury against his clients.

SIX IMPORTANT QUESTIONS TO CONSIDER

Before any boy decides his appearance is not important, he should first ask himself these 6 questions:

1. Will the way I dress make a difference in the way I feel about myself?

2. Will the way I dress affect my attitude toward others?
3. Will the clothes I wear have a bearing on the type of friends I attract?
4. Will the clothes I wear affect my emotional outlook?
5. Will the clothes I wear affect my moral behavior?
6. Will the clothes I wear affect my witness for the Lord?

Divide your class into several "buzz groups." Appoint a leader for each group. Provide each leader with a copy of one or more of the above questions to discuss. Allow 3 to 5 minutes. Then have each leader report the conclusions reached by his group.

NOTE: If the "buzz groups" arrive at conclusions you cannot agree with, listen openly to their opinions. Then simply say, "I can see how you might reach these conclusions, yet on the other hand . . ." and proceed to present alternative ideas for their consideration.

1. Will the way I dress make a difference in the way I feel about myself?

A person's appearance plays a large part in determining the kind of self-image he holds. It's impossible to look at yourself in the mirror without feeling some kind of inward response. When you look respectable, your self-image rises. You feel a greater degree of self-respect and self-confidence. On the other hand, if you see a disreputable-looking character in your mirror, your self-image plunges! Your "psyche" is convinced you are indeed a disreputable character — just like you look! If you want to feel good about yourself, you must not only **be** good but you must also **look good!**

2. Will the way I dress affect my attitude toward others?

Someone has said, **"When I hate the way I'm dressed, I hate everybody!"**

When you know your appearance is poor, you tend to withdraw. You hide away in a corner. You clam up. If a proper social attitude toward others is important, so is a proper appearance. They go together!

3. Will the kind of clothes I wear have a bearing on the type of friends I attract?

An old adage states that **"birds of feather flock together."** If you clothe yourself in the "feathers" of a certain gang of "birds," they'll naturally flock around you! But the "birds" that migrate toward you will expect you to "migrate with them" and do the things they do. If you want to attract the kids that travel the high road, dress like them! If you want to attract the kids that follow a muddy trail, dress like them!

4. Will the clothes I wear affect my emotional outlook?

Clothes will affect your emotional attitudes — for good or for bad! A sharp-looking outfit will help you feel sharp. A dull, drab outfit will help you feel dull and drab — just like you look! The Bible declares that a merry heart is as beneficial as medicine! (See Prov. 17:22.) If it's important to keep your spirits high, then it's also important to wear the clothes that will help you do it!

5. Will the clothes I wear affect my moral behavior?

Strangely enough, they can! There is a subtle correlation between the clothing you wear and the way you behave! Every actor, football player, soldier or band member knows this! Costumes, uniforms and other types of clothing subtly "program" a person's actions. Human beings instinctively tend to act the way they look!

This is no recent discovery. Why did savage tribes don war paint, frightful ornaments and hostile-appearing garb before going into battle against their enemies? They discovered that by looking fierce and ferocious it was easier for them to act that way, too!

Satan is also aware that clothing can influence a person's behavior. That's why he urges the "straight" kids to adopt the "uniform" of the morally lax gang. He knows that once you dress the part, it's easier to act the part! Wearing the uniform of the Godless gang helps you to slip into their mental outlook and moral behavior.

6. Will my clothing affect my witness for the Lord?

It may, for this reason: When your appearance is acceptable, your witness for Christ gains a wider and more respectful audience. When your appearance is oddball, the effectiveness of your Christian testimony is reduced.

When you wear grubby-looking clothes, you tell the world that you consider yourself unworthy of the care that any object of real value deserves. The world accepts your self-appraisal and thus dismisses you as "second-rate." And when they reject you, they reject your Christian witness as well!

If you're a Christian, it's right that you place a proper value upon yourself — not in heady pride, but in humble acknowledgement of what the Lord has done for you. If you wear a low price-tag before the world, you belittle the high price Christ paid to redeem you. If the "King of Kings" has taken up residence within your body, why not dress in a way that will honor him?

FOLLOW THESE CLOTHING RULES
(Page 55, Student's Training Manual)

1. Make sure your clothes are neat and clean.

One look at "Phoney Philip" on page 54 will convince you that neatness is essential to a good appearance. You will learn more about cleanliness and neatness in our training session on grooming.

But for the moment, let's presume that you have a closet full of clothes that are in good order. It is morning. The alarm clock has just rung. You drag yourself out of bed and stand in front of your closet wondering what to put on.

How do you decide what to wear? One question you'll want to ask yourself is this: **"What will the other kids be wearing?"** Should you follow their lead exactly? This brings us to the second rule.

2. Conform somewhat to others, but don't lose your individuality.

Yes, you'll want to look "somewhat" like the others, but be careful not to go overboard on conformity. A certain amount is desirable; otherwise you'd look peculiar. But don't conform so completely that you look exactly like every other kid in the room! If you do, you'll lose your own sharp edge — **the thing that defines you as "you."**

3. Dress appropriately for the occasion, the activity, and the role you'll be playing.

Ask yourself: "Where am I going? What will I be doing?" You'll want to wear clothes that are appropriate. This means clothing which is suitable for the occasion, the activity, and the role you'll be playing.

Would you wear bathing trunks in a snowstorm? No, it wouldn't be appropriate. Neither is it appropriate for you to attend a church wedding in faded blue jeans and tennis shoes.

Appropriate clothing is also **functional** clothing. This means that it is **practical.** It will serve you well in the activity or job you are engaged in.

If your clothing on the one hand is so tight that it limits your movements or on the other hand so loose that it gets caught in objects, your clothes are a handicap to you. They're neither functional nor sensible-looking.

Knowing what to wear **when** and **where** is not always easy. Here are some guidelines to help you:

Suggest that the students take notes on the instruction to follow. Space is provided in their Training Manuals at the bottom of page 55.

• **What to wear at school:**

Wear casual clothes. (Casual does **not** mean sloppy!) Dress with moderation. (This means no unusual get-ups.) Dress in such a way that you can function properly in the school program without undue hindrance. Dress so that your appearance does not divert attention away from the class instruction.

(Can you imagine trying to concentrate on a mathematical equation with the girl in the next seat wearing a pink ballerina outfit — or with the guy across the aisle decked out in a leopard skin?)

If your school has a dress code, **follow it!** The Bible says, "Let every soul be subject unto the higher powers" (Rom. 13:1). Obeying school laws is one way to follow this command.

- **What to wear at church:**

Show respect for God's house by wearing respectable clothes. When attending a worship service, wear the best you have (in keeping with the situation, of course). The same rule applies when you are a guest at a wedding or a reception. Show your respect for the person being honored by dressing **respectfully.**

- **How to dress when applying for a job:**

Dress moderately, neatly, and appropriately! When applying for a job in an office building, wear clothes suitable to that environment. Your prospective employer may want to see how you would look as an office boy, clerk or messenger. When applying for a job that involves dirty manual labor, however, don't wear your dirty old "grubbies." Wear clean, casual clothes, but never your Sunday best!

- **How to dress for a date:**

First, dress quietly. Girls don't like to be seen with a fellow who looks loud and conspicuous. If you let your clothes take over and cry for attention, you may end up next time crying for a date!

Secondly, try to appear **"in step"** with her. If she dresses exquisitely for the date and you appear in jeans and sweat shirt, she'll feel embarrassed and "let down." Girls usually like to look nice more often than boys. Give your date a chance to do so. When a girl accepts your invitation, simply ask, "Do you want to dress up or shall we go casual?"

Trying to appear **in step** with her does not mean that you have to dress **like** her! Avoid the "his and her" outfits that make you look like a "her." The uni-sex look does not find its roots in the Bible. On the contrary, God's Word says that a man should not put on the clothing of a woman. (See Deut. 22:5.) And doesn't this make sense? No normal guy would want to blur the dividing line between the sexes, for that would detract from the very thing he admires most in girls — the fact that they're **opposite** from him — in other words, their **femininity.**

When going on a first-time date, avoid wearing brand-new clothes, (unless, of course, you have nothing else to wear). On a first-time date you may tend to feel slightly self-conscious. If you're decked out in clothes you've never worn before, you may feel doubly self-conscious. And if you're so aware of your new clothes that you can't get your mind off **yourself**, you're sure to be a flop as a companion!

- **How to dress for dinner at a restaurant:**

A popular folk song says, "All God's children got shoes!" You've got them — **so wear them.** When eating with others, courtesy demands that you avoid barrenness of any kind. Hairy chests, bare legs or bare feet are definitely out of place.

Let the degree of formality of the restaurant itself (as well as the occasion) dictate your choice of clothes. If you'll be seated at a table with a white linen tablecloth, you should probably wear your best.

4. Become color-wise. Wear brighter colors in smaller doses, and only one vivid color at a time.

Don't combine vivid colors. Pants of a strong shade of blue or green, for example, will not look good when combined with a shirt of vivid red or orange. For more pleasing results, combine two shades of the same color — for example, a light blue shirt with dark blue pants.

Remember also: The brighter the color, the less pleasing it is in large doses. Use moderation with intense colors not only because of their visual effect but also because of their psychological effect upon others. To wear clothes of extreme or uncommon colors is like wearing a sign that says, "Hey! **Look at me!** I'm so great that I deserve attention!" Earn your attention by the kind of fellow you **are** — not by the bright colors you wear!

5. Key your shoes to the color of your pants. Key your socks to the color of your shoes or your pants.

Brown shoes are best with brown pants, but you may wear either brown or black shoes with pants of other colors. For the most pleasing effect, match the color of your socks either with the color of your shoes or with the color of your pants. Do not introduce a third color in your socks.

6. Coordinate your outfits with care. Do not combine more than 2 patterns in your basic apparel items.

You may see men wearing bold prints, plaids, checks and stripes — and combining them wildly! If you want to be certain of presenting a **top** appearance, however, pay attention to the standard rules of pattern combination.

Refer students to "How to Combine Patterns," on page 56 of the Student's Training Manual.

Do not combine more than 2 patterns in your basic items of clothing. Your basic items are (1) your pants, (2) your shirt, and (3) your jacket. (Included under the category of "jacket" is any other apparel item worn over your shirt, such as a sweater or vest.)

- If your pants and shirt are both patterned, choose a jacket of solid color.

- If your jacket and pants are both patterned, choose a shirt of solid color.

- If your jacket and shirt are both patterned, choose pants of solid color.

You may see this rule broken today. For example, a fellow may be found wearing a plaid jacket with checkerboard pants and a flowered shirt. But the picture he presents is a disturbing one. The more striking the various patterns that are involved, the more displeasing are the results when this rule is broken.

In choosing your accessories — ties, belts, socks — seek to contrast your patterned items with plain ones.

Call attention to the examples given in the Student's Training Manual, page 56.

If you invite a "guest-expert" for this session, ask him to bring various items of boy's apparel to provide the students with good examples of color coordination and pattern combinations.

Suggest also that he instruct the class on how to recognize a well-made item of apparel by the firm stitching, wide seams, and other neat tailoring details.

7. Choose the right line, color and pattern for your build.

Refer students to the illustrations on page 56 of their Training Manuals.

Boys come in various shapes and sizes. Some are king-sized while others are mini-size. Of course, lazy fat may be trimmed away (as you learned in our sessions on diet and exercise), but some physical features are unchangeable. If you're tall, **you're tall.** And if you're short, **you're short.** The Bible states it this way: "Which of you by taking thought can add one cubit unto his stature" (Matt. 6:27)? Your bone structure, whether you approve of it or not, is here to stay!

By learning a few simple techniques, however, you can create an **"illusion"** of a different body height or breadth. The human eye naturally follows lines. If you wear up-and-down lines, the eye senses height. If you wear side-ways lines, the eye senses width. The eye is also attracted to light and dark colors. Light colors accentuate your proportions and dark colors minimize them.

Refer students to page 56 of their Training Manuals, "If You're Tall and Slim" and "If You're Short and Chubby." Read the various items "to wear" and the items "to avoid wearing" under each category.

After you have learned how to choose the proper clothing for your body-build, the next step is to forget about your stature problems. Accept yourself **as you are,** for God has made you **as you are:** "Shall the thing formed say to him that formed it, Why hast thou made me thus" (Rom. 9:20)?

Don't allow an unalterable abundance or scarcity of inches in any direction to make you feel self-conscious or resentful. The apostle Paul had a "thorn in the flesh," but he lived as triumphantly as any mortal man ever lived! God has a purpose for your life. He can use you **just as you** are for his glory!

WHY DO WE WEAR CLOTHES?

Some of you may be thinking, "Wouldn't it be easier if we didn't have to wear clothes at all?"

Why **do** we wear clothes? **Animals don't.** Why is man the **only** creature that wears clothes? Why didn't God provide man with some kind of natural covering to keep his body warm? He gave the animals their fur covering and the birds their feathers. **Why was man left out?**

This is a good question to ask the evolutionists! According to their theory of adaptation, man shouldn't **have** to wear clothes. By now, he should have developed an excellent covering for his body — one perfectly suited to his environment. But here again, the theory of evolution leads to a dead end road. To find out why man wears clothes, we must turn to the Bible.

Man has not always worn clothes.

In the beginning, the scriptures tell us, Adam and Eve wore no clothes. The Bible says, "They were both naked, the man and his wife, and were not ashamed" (Gen. 2:25).

It is interesting to note that Adam and Eve, at this period of unashamed nakedness, possessed a unique relationship with God. Made in the image of God — and with that image yet unmarred by sin — they were clothed in innocency. Some feel they may have been surrounded by a radiant light of God similar to his shekinah glory. We do not know. But whatever their condition, they felt no lack.

No storms and no thorns!

Adam and Eve's nakedness was completely compatible with the perfect environment they enjoyed in the garden of Eden. They needed no protection from thorns or thistles, wind or rain storms, **for there were none!** The earth had not yet fallen under the curse that came as a result of man's fall.

Man sins and suffers loss.

One day sin entered, and we find Adam and Eve looking at each other, aware for the first time that they both were naked. Realizing they had suffered a great loss in the loss of their innocency, the two attempted to atone for it by making a hasty fig leaf covering. Therefore we see that the **first act of man** following man's **first act** of sin was to make man's **first suit of clothes!**

And man ever since has been covering his nakedness! The roots of today's gigantic clothing industry lie in the fall of man in the garden of Eden, for **clothing entered the world when sin entered!**

Satan wants man either to "undress" or to "overdress."

Satan, who instigated the first sin, is still trying to slither into the act. Because clothing is a reminder of man's fall, Satan encourages the cult of nudity. He knows that the man who espouses nudity in essence is saying: "I am **not** a fallen creature! There is nothing higher from whence I came! I need **no covering**, for I have incurred **no shame!** I am no different from an animal! And if animals need no clothes, **neither do I!"**

If this plan of Satan fails, and he cannot induce man to **"undress"** — then he encourages him to **"overdress"**! And so we see false ostentation . . . over-adornment of the body . . . the worship of clothes! Whereas clothing was originally a mark of man's **shame,** Satan tempts man to use clothing as a vehicle for human **pride** and self-exaltation.

Adam and Eve felt no pride — only gratitude.

When Adam and Eve donned the coats of skin God gave them, they felt only humility and gratitude for God's provisions. For in receiving these clothes they were confessing they had a need. They were acknowledging the fact that they lacked something that must be provided for them by another. In order to receive their coats of skin, an animal had to die for them. **Blood had to be shed for them!** A beautiful picture of what took place hundreds of years later when Jesus Christ, the Lamb of God, **shed his blood** to provide man a **covering for his sin.**

Each of us needs a covering for our sin.

When we receive this sacrifice of the Son of God offered on our behalf, God no longer sees our "shame and nakedness." Instead, he sees us covered by Christ's spotless robe of righteousness. The Bible says, "He hath made him (Jesus) to be sin for us . . . that we might be made the righteousness of God in him" (2 Cor. 5:21).

Some day we'll stand before God! What will we wear then? The only garment fit for Heaven will be the robe of righteousness provided by the Lord Jesus Christ!

DOES "BELONGING TO CHRIST" MAKE A DIFFERENCE IN THE WAY A YOUNG MAN DRESSES?
(Page 57, Student's Training Manual)

Read and discuss these 10 points with your students.

Prayer:

Father, may we honor you in the way we clothe our bodies. And may we please you by receiving with grateful hearts the robe of righteousness freely offered through the shed blood of your Son, Jesus Christ. Amen.

Memory Question No. 9: Why do we need Christ's spotless robe of righteousness upon us?

Answer: "We are all as an unclean thing, and all our righteousnesses are as filthy rags" (Isa. 64:6).

UNDERSTANDING SEX MORALITY

(Pages 58 — 61, Student's Training Manual)

Note: Present those portions of the following material which are appropriate for your particular class of boys depending upon their age and degree of maturity. Inasmuch as the material presented herein deals primarily with Biblical sex morality, the parents of your students will undoubtedly be grateful for the support your instruction provides.

In this lesson, as in some of the others, you may wish to schedule a guest speaker such as a medical doctor or a Christian counselor to add further interest.

THINKING ABOUT SEX IS NORMAL
If you're like most boys, you've spent some time thinking about sex. You've been curious about girls. You've speculated about the meaning of love and marriage. You've been exposed to many different ideas concerning sex, love and marriage. You've wondered which are trustworthy and which are not. Above all, you've wanted to know the truth.

ATTITUDES TOWARD SEX VARY GREATLY
In some circles you may have noticed a "hush, hush" attitude toward sex, as though the subject were too shameful or too embarassing to talk about! In other groups you've noticed fellows directing every conversation toward sex as though it were the most important thing in a boy's life!

YOU MUST MAKE YOUR OWN DECISIONS
As you've observed and pondered these differing attitudes, you've come to realize that you, as a young man, must make your own personal decisions about sex. You must decide how you should view this force within your body, what attitudes you should hold concerning it, and what guidelines you should follow.

FOR EXAMPLE...
- Are you going to view your sex drive as simply another biological phenomenon like hunger or thirst, or as something far more meaningful than that?
- Will you consider your sex urges as something to be satisfied now, or something to be diverted until later?

- Whose advice will you seek and follow in regard to your sexual conduct? Your parents' or the kids' down the street?

TWO BOYS WITH A HIGH-POWERED MACHINE

As you consider these questions, your dilemma could be compared to that of a boy and his younger brother who've been presented a uniquely-designed, high-powered machine. They view it with mixed delight and awe, for they know it holds great potential either to benefit or to destroy their lives — as well as the lives of others!

"Wow!" says the younger brother. "What a machine! Let's give it a try right now!"

"Hold on there," cautions the older boy. "First, we'd better gather some facts on how to operate the thing!"

"Where'll we find information like that?" asks the younger boy. He looks around the room. "Here's Mom's recipe book! Will that help?"

"Ridiculous!" snorts the older brother.

"Well . . . how about this World Travel Guide? Or maybe the Telephone Directory?"

"That's crazy!" retorts the older boy. "We need to look in the Instruction Manual! That's the only reliable guide! It's written by the man who designed the machine! Who'd know more about how to handle it than he would?"

"Hmmm . . . maybe you're right," acknowledges the younger brother. Together they examine the manual accompanying the machine.

In a few minutes the younger boy speaks indignantly. "Throw that book out!" he yells. "Look at all those silly restrictions! Don't do this . . . and don't do that! That designer's nothing but a 'kill-joy'!" In anger he starts to toss the Instruction Manual into the trash basket.

The older boy grabs it back. "Don't be a dummy!" he explodes. "What makes you think the designer'd be working against us?"

"Read the instructions! See for yourself!" replies the younger brother. "It's obvious he's trying to spoil our fun!"

"Why would he want to do that? Why do you think he engineered this thing in the first place — to make our lives miserable? Of course, not!

He gave us this machine to make our lives more enjoyable! He's not trying to deprive us of anything good with those restrictions! He's just trying to save us from the problems we'd face if we'd use our machine the wrong way!"

The younger boy broods quietly for a moment. Then he stubbornly insists, "I still say it's our machine . . . and we ought to be able to use it any way we want!"

"Yeah . . . and mess up our lives . . . and maybe some other people's, too? Is that what you want? Get smart, kid! We can't go wrong if we follow the instructions exactly like they're written in the book . . . and we're sure to get a lot more satisfaction out of our machine in the long run!"

Ask your students: Which boy had the right idea? Why? Discuss briefly; then help your students apply this story to their own lives by reading aloud the following questions:

1. Who designed you as a sexual being and placed this dynamic creative force within you?

2. Is it reasonable that your Designer and Maker would leave you without directions regarding the powerful "sex machinery" he's placed within you?

3. Where can you find such directions? What constitutes your "Instruction Manual"?

4. Why has your Designer given you the precautions and restrictions you find in your "Instruction Manual"? Is he trying to make your life miserable? Is he "for" you or "against" you?

5. Why do some guys end up with sex-damaged lives? Have they heeded the "Instruction Manual," or have they followed other sources of information which are no more authoritative on the subject than your Mom's cook-book, or the World Travel Guide, or the Telephone Directory?

Point out that boys often foolishly base their important life-decisions regarding sex on what "the boy next door" says, or on the tainted lives portrayed on the television or movie screen, or on the lurid misinformation set forth in pornographic literature.

Emphasize the fact that the Bible is our only trustworthy guide. Written by the Author and Designer of sex himself, it constitutes our "Instruction Manual."

SCRIPTURAL GUILDELINES FOR CHRISTIAN BOYS
(Pages 58 and 59, Student's Training Manual)

Ten questions regarding basic sex principles are listed here, together with the answers based on God's Word. Read each question aloud. Have your students enter the missing words after referring to the scripture verses given.

GOD'S WORD SAYS . . .
(Page 59, Student's Training Manual)

Discuss with your students the following instructions and warnings from God's Word:

FLEE FORNICATION. FLEE ALSO YOUTHFUL LUSTS.
God promises to provide a way to escape every temptation. (See 1 Cor. 10:13.) But the way of escape he provides may be **total flight** as it was for Joseph! (Read Gen. 39:2-12.)

A harmless "kitty"?
Let's take a look at the cartoon strip on page 59 in our Training Manuals. Fornication (or sex sin) often appears as harmless as the "kitty" we see sitting under the tree in the first illustration. Because of the kitty's pleasing appearance, this fellow decides it's nothing to be afraid of. Even though he may have been warned about this kind of temptation, he's confident "he can handle it!"

The "kitty" has tiger teeth!
While **appearing** to shun outright involvement with sex sin, this fellow actually **invites** it by his actions and thoughts (as we see in the second illustration).

What is the result? The last picture shows us. Too late the fellow discovers that the innocent-appearing "kitty" has the **teeth of a tiger!** Too late he wishes he'd followed God's warning to "flee fornication"!

KEEP THYSELF PURE. WHATSOEVER THINGS ARE PURE . . . THINK ON THESE THINGS.
Notice that the Bible tells you to **keep yourself** pure. In other words, **you are the one to do the "keeping"!** Others may try to help you stay pure, but ultimately **you** are the one who makes the choices that determine your purity!

Social conventions once imposed helpful restraints.

In former days, society attempted to keep unmarried young people sexually pure by subjecting them to a strict code of social conventions. For example, a fellow was not allowed to be alone with a young lady without a chaperone present, or at least a watchful adult nearby. Much less would he have been given the keys to the family car!

Many protective "side-rails" have been removed.

These strict conventions protected young people from exposure to sexual temptations in the same way that side-rails protect a pedestrian from slipping off a footbridge. Society today, however, has removed many of these protective "side-rails" and it's up to you — more than ever — to keep **yourself** pure, as the Bible says.

How can you do it? **By providing your own protective "side-rails"!** Here are some precautionary measures which will keep you from falling off that precarious bridge that a boy must pass over on his way from childhood to manhood.

HOW TO BUILD YOUR OWN PROTECTION AGAINST SLIPPING:

When you're on a date, stay active, and stay with others!

Don't allow too much time alone with a girl with nothing to do! Plan your time together so that it is filled with absorbing, wholesome activities. Invite other young persons to share these activities with you. This provides an excellent protective "side-rail." Take advantage of it!

Don't lower your inhibitions and dull your judgment (or your conscience) by drinking alcoholic beverages.

Drinkers often lament, **"I couldn't help what happened! I was drinking!"** But God does not absolve an intoxicated person from personal guilt.

If you choose to deaden the God-given higher faculties of your soul, and allow judgment, conscience, reason and self-control to be temporarily placed out of commission, you are actually saying, **"I do not care what happens!"** You are deliberately choosing to throttle your higher nature and to allow your lower nature full control. God cannot in justice hold you guiltless.

During your teen years you particularly need the help of God-implanted restraints and inhibitions to prevent disasters and life-long scars. **Drinking and dating invite sexual disaster!** Keep your mental faculties in good shape! Now is the time you need this "protective side-rail" the most!

Don't allow your mind to get "all tied up" with sex!

Instead, "sublimate" or "divert" your sex drive by channeling your thoughts into other interests. Pursue some absorbing hobby or endeavor. Set up some challenging worthwhile goals!

Diverting your interest away from sex may at first require definite effort (for sex is one of the easiest things for a boy to become interested in), but don't give up! As you continue to take determined steps to center your thoughts elsewhere, other interests **will** move in, take root and grow. Sublimation has been the answer for many fellows. **It's one of the strongest protective "bridge-rails" a fellow can build for himself.** Try it . . . you'll see it works!

THOU SHALT NOT COMMIT ADULTERY. WHOSOEVER LOOKETH ON A WOMAN TO LUST AFTER HER HATH COMMITTED ADULTERY WITH HER ALREADY IN HIS HEART.

Looking at a woman for the express purpose of feeding improper sex desires is against God's law. In other words, **if your "looking" is for the purpose of "lusting," it is wrong!**

But what about the unexpected view of an alluring female flashed on the television screen? Or the unavoidable observation of a shapely girl in a bathing suit? Such inescapable sights are not what Jesus is condemning in Matthew 5:28. Rather it is the **gloating gaze** that a fellow might **voluntarily prolong** to feed his wrong desires.

Avoid self-defeating behavior.

"But," you might say, "I like to look at girls! It's a pleasant sort of thing! Can't I ever look at a girl twice?"

Of course, you can — just so long as your prolonged looking does not foster unwholesome thoughts! (You, yourself, will have to gauge your reactions.) But common sense will tell you that dwelling on the feminine form won't make your "sublimation job" any easier! **Why work against yourself?** Would you practice this kind of self-defeating behavior in other areas of your life?

Self-defeating behavior indicates insincerity.

Let's say, for example, that your doctor places you on a strict "no-sweets-allowed" diet for a serious matter of health. Would you spend all your spare time gazing through bakery windows . . . gloating over the frosting swirls . . . trying to imagine exactly how each "goodie" might taste if you had one in your mouth? One thing is sure — the fellow who does this is not truly sincere in his efforts to stay on his diet!

NEITHER FORNICATORS . . . NOR ADULTERERS, NOR EFFEMINATE, NOR ABUSERS OF THEMSELVES WITH MANKIND . . . SHALL INHERIT THE KINGDOM OF GOD.

When God removed "woman" from "man," in a sense he created a vacuum. Just as a vacuum seeks to be filled, so human beings seek fulfillment through union with the opposite sex. Man is missing that part of him which was removed when woman was made. Therefore man is attracted to woman. Woman likewise senses that she is only part of the whole and that man is essential to her completeness. Therefore woman is attracted to man.

Sex hunger is to be satisfied through physical union of man and woman in marriage.

Since God created man's sex hunger by the physical **separation** of woman from man, God plans for man's sex hunger to be satisfied by the physical **re-uniting** of woman to man as it occurs in marriage. For human beings to attempt to gratify their sexual hunger in any other way is a deviation from God's plan. This would include any man-to-man sexual gratification such as occurs in homosexuality or any self-stimulated gratification such as occurs in masturbation.

Self-abuse is a misuse of sex.

Any such deviation from the man-woman sexual relationship is a **misuse or abuse** of the sex nature God has implanted within human beings. This is why the Bible refers to homosexuals as **"abusers" of themselves with mankind.**

The practice of masturbation likewise has long been recognized as **"self-abuse."** One of the hazards of masturbation is that those who practice **"self"**-abuse are in greater danger of becoming "abusers of themselves **with mankind."** Masturbation can lead in the direction of homosexuality.

Homosexual acts are sin.

Though some today would have us believe that homosexual activity is neither wrong nor immoral (but simply a different life-style), God's Word (our Instruction Manual) declares that it is sin. The Bible tells us that God's judgment on the cities of Sodom and Gomorrah (because of their widespread practice of homosexuality) was to serve as a warning to all who might live ungodly lives thereafter. (See 2 Peter 2:6.)

Homosexuality therefore is not a practice to be joked about, or to be shrugged off lightly as simply another personal preference as inconsequential as preferring chocolate rather than vanilla ice cream. **God says homosexual acts are sin.**

Likewise, though some psychologists today are saying that masturbation is not wrong, most boys who become caught in this trap feel deep within themselves that their actions are shameful and improper.

God forgives and helps those who seek deliverance from sexual sins.

What is a fellow to do if he has fallen into wrong sexual practices? Is it possible for him to break these habits? Will God love and forgive him?

Yes! God stands ready to forgive him for past sins and to help him keep free from such sins in the future. But the fellow must be willing to do his part.

What must the fellow do?
First of all, he must acknowledge that he has done wrong. He must not whitewash or excuse his actions.

Next, he must tell God that he wants to be delivered from these sins. He must truly and sincerely desire to be set free.

Finally, he must take firm and deliberate steps to help himself become a free person.

What are these steps?

• **He must avoid any person who might lead him into temptation.**
He must cut off all companionship with persons who have been involved with him in his wrongdoing. He must form wholesome new friendships to fill this void.

• **He must avoid every situation that might lead him into temptation.**
If too much time alone with nothing to do places him in the way of temptation, he must force himself to become active in some kind of work, hobby or study. Or he should seek association with someone else (if the right kind of person is available).

• **He must avoid every book, magazine, T.V. program or movie that might prove sexually stimulating.**
Instead, he must read and memorize scripture passages — especially those portions which will provide help for him in time of temptation.

• **He must maintain a regular prayer life.**
He must practice calling upon God when sudden temptation strikes. God will answer any sincere request for help. **God wants him to win this battle!**

"But," you may ask, "what about the Bible verse that says fornicators and homosexuals won't inherit the kingdom of God?" (See 1 Cor. 6:9,10.)

Fortunately, that's not the end of the story. There is a way out! Let's read the verse which follows this statement:

> "And such were some of you: but ye are washed, but ye are sanctified, but ye are justified in the name of the Lord Jesus, and by the Spirit of our God" (1 Cor. 6:11).

Once they were trapped. Now they're set free!
Some of the very men to whom the apostle Paul was writing had previously been guilty of these same sins. (See verses 9 and 10.) But through Christ and the work of the Holy Spirit upon their lives, they had been cleansed and made acceptable in God's sight. They had received power to turn away from their sins once and for all. Paul wrote: "Such **were** some of you!" (Note the past tense.)

In other words, they no longer fit the description given in verses 9 and 10. Whereas once they had been trapped, that was now a thing of the past! They were set free! And Christ can do the same today for any fellow who has been caught in the web of these sins. The same power is available to him. He, too, can be set free!

BE NOT DECEIVED: GOD IS NOT MOCKED: FOR WHATSOEVER A MAN SOWETH, THAT ALSO SHALL HE REAP. HE THAT SOWETH TO HIS FLESH SHALL OF THE FLESH REAP CORRUPTION.
(Page 60. Student's Training Manual)

Call your students' attention to the cartoons at the top of this page.

God's physical laws bring consequences.
God has ordained that his creation be governed by a vast number of natural and physical laws. Fighting or flouting these laws is futile, for they continue to operate whether you like them or not! Intelligent people plan their lives so as to cooperate with God's physical laws. Before taking any action, they consider the natural consequences of that action. **If they don't like the consequences, they avoid the action!**

God's moral laws bring consequences, also.

Our universe is more than a physical universe. We live in a moral universe as well — one which is controlled by **unchanging** moral laws. Just as intelligent people plan their lives to cooperate with God's physical laws, so they also plan their lives to cooperate with God's moral laws. Before taking any moral action, they consider the consequences of that action. **If they don't like the consequences, they avoid the action!**

What are the consequences of sexual immorality?

Sexual immorality produces guilt, shame, loss of self-esteem, psychological and emotional problems. Sexual immorality can **never** produce happiness, because it is in direct conflict with God's unchanging moral law.

The Bible says that sin brings its own judgment down upon our heads. "His own iniquities shall take the wicked himself, and he shall be holden with the cords of his sins" (Prov. 5:22). An evil act inflicts its own punishment upon the wrongdoer, for a law of recompense exists in this world.

Laughing at God's laws doesn't stop their operation.

The Bible says that God is "not mocked." This means that those who ridicule or laugh at God's laws will still find themselves subject to them.

Refer students again to the cartoons at the top of page 60.

You will notice that the fellow who disregarded one of God's physical laws (by sitting too close to the window ledge) subsequently suffered the consequences of his carelessness (as we see in the middle illustration). What about the fellow in the last illustration? Evidently he has flouted one of God's moral laws. Will he go free?

No! Puny human beings cannot laugh off God's moral laws without suffering the consequences any more than they can his physical laws! Why not? **Because God is not a fool. He is not powerless and ineffective. He is holy. He is just. His laws are exacting and unchanging.**

Even "forgiven sins" may leave scars.

"But," you might ask, "if Jesus took our punishment on the cross, why do we still have to suffer if we break God's laws?"

True, when we trust Christ as our Saviour, our sins are forgiven and we are assured a place in Heaven eternally. But sin, by its very nature, brings misery and regret. Some sins, though forgiven, leave scars that we must carry as long as we remain on earth.

For example: A man who engages in promiscuous sex may repent and be eternally forgiven. God will never hold this sin against him again. But this will not prevent his developing a crippling venereal disease as a consequence of that sin.

Likewise, a boy who impregnates a girl may repent and be forgiven. Nevertheless this will not prevent an illegitimate child from being born as a consequence of that sin.

Reaping comes later.

Perhaps you're thinking, "But I know some guys who've done plenty of wrong things, and they seem to be getting by O.K."

It may **appear** that way right now. But remember: **A time element is always involved between the season of sowing and the season of reaping.** Does a farmer sow his seeds in the morning and reap his crop in the afternoon? No! Neither does a fellow who sows sin always reap sin's harvest immediately.

Furthermore, the guy who appears to be suffering no ill effects from his wrongdoings **may only appear to be doing well.** A clever fellow can hide his feelings. He may laugh. He may joke. But deep inside he may be fighting guilt, fears, loss of self-respect and tormenting memories. This is the "soul-damage" that accompanies sin. The Bible says, "Whoso committeth adultery with a woman ... **destroyeth his own soul.** A wound and dishonour shall he get and his reproach shall not be wiped away" (Prov. 6:32,33).

How can a good gift harm lives?

Some of you may be thinking: "Sex sure does cause a lot of problems! If it's such a good gift of God, why does it create so much unhappiness in the world?"

Consider these questions:

Is food a good gift of God? Yes! But when an individual becomes gluttonous, he may eat himself to death!

Is water a good gift of God? Yes! But when an individual fails to respect its properties, he may drown in it!

Is fire a good gift of God? Yes! But when an individual uses it carelessly, he may be burned by it!

Every good gift of God remains good only so long as it is rightly used within the framework and limitations of God's physical and moral laws.

Is sex a good gift of God? Yes! But when an individual uses it outside the limits of marriage as ordained of God, he brings deep injury not only upon his own life but also upon the lives of others!

Is sexual repression harmful?

Some guys excuse their sexual immorality by declaring that it's harmful to repress the sex drive. But psychiatrists and physicians tell a different story — and one which agrees with the Bible! They say that the fellows most often plagued by mental and emotional disorders (as well as certain physical disorders) are not the ones who have practiced sexual restraint. Rather they're the sexually promiscuous ones who habitually satisfy their immediate cravings with no thought of the consequences ahead.

Listening to good advice is a sign of wisdom.

Some guys boast that they want to make their own mistakes and learn their lessons **"the hard way"**!

"Don't tell me what to do!" they charge defiantly. "I'll find out for **myself**!"

But God's Word cautions against such a heady, cocksure attitude: "The way of a fool is right in his own eyes," the Bible warns, "but he that hearkeneth unto counsel is wise" (Prov. 12:15).

MARRIAGE IS HONORABLE IN ALL

Immediately after originating sex and thereby creating a state of "incompleteness" in both man and woman, God instituted marriage as the answer to this condition of "incompleteness."

In arithmetic, 1 + 1 = 2. But in God's "marriage arithmetic," one + one = one! The Bible says, "For this cause shall a man leave his father and mother, and shall be joined unto his wife, and they two shall be one flesh" (Eph. 5:31).

How can two possibly become one?

Two can become one only when each is an incomplete part or "fraction" of the whole. This is true of both man and woman. Each needs the other in order to become entire and whole. Each lacks what the other supplies.

Man and woman, though **similar** to each other, are also at the same time **opposite** from each other — just as a concave and convex surface are at once both similar and opposite. Yet it is this same "similar and opposite" design that peculiarly enables them to fit together as **one** forming a perfect whole!

Sex difference is more than physical.

Men and women are designed by God not only to complement each other physically but also temperamentally and emotionally. For example:

- **Whereas man is more agressive,** woman is more content to follow.
- **Whereas man enjoys the role of the "protector,"** woman takes joy in being protected.

- **Whereas man is more firm and forceful in speech and manner,** woman is more soft and gentle.

- **Whereas man is more likely to make decisions by means of logical analysis,** woman is more likely to be influenced by an emotional appeal or to forsake all reason and follow her "womanly intuition."

- **Whereas man is more inclined to be authoritarian and domineering,** woman is more docile and submissive.

- **Whereas man is more suspicious and questioning,** woman is more easily beguiled.

- **Whereas man is more greatly impressed with action and accomplishment,** woman is more deeply affected by romance and beauty, culture and refinement, or the so-called "niceties" of life.

- **Whereas man's manner is more harsh and gruff,** woman's manner is more mild and delicate.

- **Whereas man's broad shoulders and strong hands are designed to perform heavy tasks,** (to labor and build and thus to enable him to be the provider), a woman's physique is uniquely designed to perform the functions and tasks of motherhood.

Woman is at her best when displaying tenderness and tact; when soothing and pleasing others; when caring for the helpless, the needy, the lonely, the hungry, the weak; when giving comfort and encouragement — in short, when "mothering."

What one lacks the other supplies.

What man lacks, he finds in woman! What woman lacks, she finds in man! When God made man and woman similar yet opposite (and thus complementary to each other), he knew exactly what he was doing. It was all part of his plan to provide the most complete, harmonious and satisfying relationship possible for both man and woman as they are joined in marriage as lifelong companions, helpers and co-partners in the rearing and nurturing of children in the home.

MARRIAGE BENEFITS BOTH MAN AND SOCIETY

"Wherefore they are no more twain, but one flesh. What therefore God hath joined together, let not man put asunder" (Matt. 19:5,6).

"Marriage is honorable in all, and the bed undefiled: but whoremongers and adulterers God will judge" (Heb. 13:4).

Today some make light of the marriage relationship. But when God instituted marriage, he knew what was best not only for man but also for society. What would be the result if unlimited sex freedom became the rule?

At one time during the Russian Revolution, an attempt was made to destroy the Biblical concept of marriage and family. Legal restraints against free love were removed. Premarital sex, rather than being condemned, was given outright approval and even encouragement by the state.

The results of these decrees were so ruinous that the government soon discovered that the strength of the nation was being destroyed. Therefore it issued a new policy statement declaring that the state could not exist without the family, and that chastity before marriage as well as lifelong commitment in marriage was to be practiced, inasmuch as it was highly beneficial to the state.

Atheistic Russia — even while refusing to acknowledge God — was forced to return to the sex and marriage standards set forth in God's Word, proving once again that **God is not mocked!** His moral laws cannot be broken without dire consequences to both man and society.

HOW DOES A FELLOW HONOR THE STATE OF MARRIAGE?

"Marriage is honorable in all." When God tells us in his Word that marriage is "honorable," what does that mean? It means that marriage is worthy of respect and reverence. It is not to be treated lightly but is to be held in high esteem.

How does a fellow honor the state of marriage?

A fellow honors marriage . . .

by saving himself exclusively for the girl he will someday marry — just as he expects her to save herself exclusively for him.

A fellow honors marriage . . .

by viewing it as something set apart, something sacred and special — a rite granting him a special place of privilege.

A fellow honors marriage . . .

by keeping the line between the unmarried state and the married state drawn distinct and clear:

- Now it can be **yours!** Yesterday it was something **to look forward to!**

- Now you are **permitted** to partake of this uniquely "total" relationship! Yesterday you were **forbidden!**

- Now you are to be **one flesh!** Yesterday you were **two!**

- Now you will **know!** Yesterday you could only **wonder!**

Entering into marriage means either all of this or nothing at all!

The delight, the joy, the happiness experienced in being married is greater because of the awe, the wonder and the mystery of the waiting period preceding the event. To sneak backstage before the performance is to ruin the moment when the houselights are dimmed and the curtain goes up. To peek into your Christmas gifts before Christmas is to deprive yourself of that special glow accompanying the ceremony around the tree.

Marriage is to be a gateway.

A fellow honors marriage by looking upon it as a sacred gateway through which he enters a heretofore unexperienced relationship . . .

"Now I shall have her as my **own**! This territory I have never before intruded upon — but now it is to be **mine**! The 'no trespassing' signs have been removed, and I may 'go in unto' my wife. Today I may give my **total manhood** to this one whom God has given to me to love, protect and cherish throughout our lifetime together."

To have experienced a sexual relationship with a girl prior to marriage destroys the significance of the event. No longer is it a mystery to be unfolded. To act as though it is, makes the ceremony a sham and a mockery.

To truly honor marriage is to protect its significance by preserving one's wedding day as a day of unique revelation and discovery. According to marriage counselors, honoring marriage in this way produces the happiest marriages.

You can't "play" now without paying later!

Some boys falsely believe they can play around before marriage and then settle down to become faithful husbands. Oftentimes, however, they find that promiscuity has become a habit. They quickly become dissatisfied in an exclusive commitment to one partner.

Sexual activity before marriage has another serious after-effect. If a wife discovers that her husband engaged in sex relations with girls before she married him, she may cease to trust and respect him. When a wife's trust and respect go, her love may also go. She may find her affection straying toward someone other than her husband.

For the same reason a boy should be cautious about entering into marriage with a girl who has been promiscuous with other fellows before marriage. He, too, may find it difficult to maintain proper respect and love for his mate. A broken marriage, a broken home, and emotionally upset children may follow.

Some losses — though regretted — can never be regained.

Remember it takes but **one foolish act** to destroy your "virginity." Once lost, it can **never** be regained. Could Esau regain his birthright after he exchanged it for a momentary gratification of his physical hunger? Listen to what the Bible says:

"Lest there be any fornicator, or profane person as Esau, who for one morsel of meat sold his birthright. For ye know how that afterward, when he would have inherited the blessing, he was rejected; for he found no place of repentance though he sought it carefully with tears" (Heb. 12:16,17). Esau's bitter regrets could never bring back his birthright.

Refer your students to the illustration at the bottom of page 60. Have the class silently read the paragraph entitled "A Solemn Pledge."

CHOOSE THE FUTURE YOU WANT
(Page 61, Student's Training Manual)

Consider together the 9 choices shown here. Discuss the two columns entitled "Here's How to Get the Future You Chose." Help your students realize that their present attitudes, thoughts and actions determine their future happiness or unhappiness. Read together the 6 steps a boy should take if he is already guilty of misconduct. Emphasize God's love and forgiveness. Make it very clear to your students that with God's help a clean, new future can await such a one.

Prayer:
Lord, may we be men that are in command of our bodies. May we, like Joseph, have the strength to flee from temptation not only that we might find happiness in this life, but also that we might stand before you unashamed one day because our lives have honored the name of your Son, Jesus Christ. Amen.

Memory Question No. 10: Will we be held accountable for our moral behavior in this life?

Answer: "We must all appear before the judgment seat of Christ; that every one may receive the things done in his body, according to that he hath done, whether it be good or bad" (2 Cor. 5:10).

Note: Are there boys in your class who do not know Christ as their Saviour? You may want to schedule personal conferences with each student before the end of this course. A personal conference will afford an excellent opportunity to discuss any spiritual problems or personal needs the boy may have in his life, and to present Jesus Christ as Saviour and Helper.

OVERCOMING SELF-CONSCIOUSNESS

(Pages 62 — 67 Student's Training Manual)

YOU WILL NEED: A man's wrist watch for demonstration (see page 165.)

BEFORE YOUR CLASS BEGINS: Remove page 221, cutting on dotted lines as shown to provide parts for skit. Select 5 boys to take part in the skit and briefly review instructions with them.

Choose students who feel relaxed in front of others. Encourage them to portray their characters with appropriate posture, gestures, and facial expression. (See page 161.)

SELF-CONSCIOUSNESS HANDICAPS YOUR WORK FOR GOD

- Do social situations scare you?
- Do you often feel miserable and awkward around others?
- Do you hate to meet new people?

If so, you're like many other teenage boys, but you don't have to stay that way! A sure-fire remedy awaits you — and the "man in demand" is the one who has found it!

"But," you may ask, "what does this have to do with becoming God's man for today?"

Plenty! Can you imagine yourself going out to change the world with ropes tied around your hands and feet? **Hardly!** But in the same way a self-conscious, red-faced Christian is handicapped in his outreach for Christ. Satan has him tied up in self-conscious fears. **He cannot step out for God!**

SELF-CONSCIOUSNESS TAKES YOUR EYES OFF GOD — AND OFF OTHERS!

When you are self-conscious, you are thinking primarily about your "self." You are wide-awake to your own small self but sound asleep to your big, powerful God. This makes you feel inadequate — **and you are!** For Jesus said, **"Without me, you can do nothing."** (See John 15:5.)

When you are self-conscious, you have 20-20 vision for your own self-interest, but are blind to the next guy's lot in life.

This makes you self-centered. And in this state, your Christian witness falls **flat**! For unless the other guy feels your interest is centered in **him**, he'll turn you off fast!

WHAT CAUSES SELF-CONSCIOUSNESS?
(Page 62, Student's Training Manual)

In order to overcome self-consciousness we need to discover what causes it! Your Training Manuals (page 62) picture five different fellows who suffer from self-consciousness — each for a different reason. Take a look at these fellows! Have you ever felt like they do? We're going to meet these five fellows and hear them describe their problems.

(Have the five students chosen prior to class come to the front of the room to read their lines.)

Here they are! Each one will introduce himself to you!

SKIT — "FIVE SELF-CONSCIOUS FELLOWS"

(1) "MR. INFERIOR"

I'm Mr. Inferior. Everyone else seems better than me. *(Hang head.)* I don't measure up to the other kids. When I'm around a big shot, he overwhelms me and I feel like a "nobody"! The big shot seems so important, I'm afraid to open my mouth. Wish I could feel self-confident like the other guys, but I guess they're just better than me! I'll probably be an awkward mess all my life! *(Shake head slowly.)* But what can I expect when I'm so inferior? *(Clasp hands in front and hang head.)*

(2) "MR. INADEQUATE"

I'm Mr. Inadequate. When I'm up against a new situation, I get flustered and embarrassed! *(Swing body in an embarrassed manner.)* I don't know how to act! *(Shuffle feet.)* I wonder if I'm saying the right thing and if I'm dressed right. *(Look down at clothes.)* I feel like I'm "on the spot," and I get so nervous I can't enjoy myself! And I can't enjoy anyone else either! Sometimes I wish I'd just stayed home because I feel so inadequate." *(Shrug shoulders. Lift hands in helpless, bewildered manner.)*

(3) "MR. FEARFUL"

I'm Mr. Fearful. What do I fear? Everything! I fear I'll look foolish or make a bad impression. *(Appear timid and frightened. Chew on fingernails.)* I'm afraid others are laughing at me behind my back. *(Twist around as though looking behind.)* I'm afraid I'll be a failure and others will reject me. And when I get scared, I can't do anything right! I stiffen up . . . *(pull up rigidly)* . . . I stumble over furniture . . . *(stumble over other foot)* . . . I blush and st-st-st-st-stam-m-mer . . . and I don't know what to do with my hands! *(Shove hands in pockets. Pull them out again. Try to hide them.)* I imagine that every eye is upon me. It ruins my fun. I'm so full of fears, I'm just plain miserable! *(Assume trembling, fearful pose similar to that in Training Manual.)*

(4) "MR. SELF-CONCERNED"

I'm Mr. Self-Concerned. I can't get my mind off myself! Sure, I'm aware the other guy is there . . . but my main concern is "What does he think of me?" *(Point to self.)* Do I wonder if anyone else is having a good time? *(Motion toward others.)* No! It's me I'm worrying about! *(Point to self again.)* Do I wonder how others feel? No! I'm too occupied with my own feelings to be concerned about theirs! I'm constantly on guard to make sure I don't "lose face"! And this keeps my eyes constantly on me! Me! Me! *(Point repeatedly toward self.)*

(5) "MR. GUILTY"

I'm Mr. Guilty. When I'm running with the wrong gang and doing things I shouldn't do . . . my conscience hurts! *(Hunch shoulders and look around uneasily.)* I've found out that when I'm doing wrong, I can't feel right. And with these bad things gnawing at my conscience, I feel ill at ease — even when I'm with the right gang! I find myself thinking, "Boy, I hope they never find out!" *(Shield face with hand, as though to hide from others.)* Or, "Would they really like me if they knew?" Putting up a false front makes me so jittery, I can't act natural. *(Shake head sadly.)* It's hard to relax and be happy when you've got a guilty conscience.

Following the skit, ask your students:

- Did you recognize "yourself" in any of these fellows?
- Have you experienced the same feelings these fellows expressed?
- Did you gain new insights as to why you feel self-conscious at certain times?

Once we become aware of what causes our self-consciousness, we're better prepared to do something about it! Our Training Manuals give us 10 principles which will help us with this problem.

PRINCIPLE NO. 1:

WHEN YOU LACK CONFIDENCE . . . STRAIGHTEN UP!
(Page 62, Student's Training Manual)

What good does it do to straighten up?

The very act of assuming a manly posture helps calm your fears. Why is a soldier so thoroughly drilled in his disciplined posture? To make him feel more confident! **By controlling his body posture, he alters his inward feelings, too!**

In a previous training session we learned that "thoughts" influence posture. For instance, if you **think** you're a failure, your brain sends **"defeat signals"** to your body, and your muscles **"act out"** the part. You hang your head! You droop! You slump! But it works the other way around too.

By controlling your body posture you control your mental outlook.

If you force yourself to take a posture of success and confidence, you replace those "fear and failure signals" with "faith and confidence" signals instead! The very act of straightening up sends a flow of optimism through you, and you tell yourself, **"No problem! I can handle this!"**

The noted psychologist, William James, declared that "actions" bring about "feelings." In other words, act the way you **want** to feel — and you **will**! Act confident and you'll **feel** confident!

Discuss briefly with your students the cartoon strip in the Training Manual (page 62) which illustrates this principle. Help them to understand that in the first instance, the fellow's doubts produced his droopy posture, and his droopy posture reinforced his doubts, making him self-conscious.

Call attention to the fact that this situation is reversible, as shown by the latter instance. Here the fellow forced himself to assume a confident posture, and his confident posture produced a confident attitude. The result? A relaxed, successful response to the situation!

PRINCIPLE NO. 2:

WHEN YOU WANT TO DISPEL SOCIAL TENSION . . . SMILE!
(Page 63, Student's Training Manual)

Why smile? Because a smile is relaxing to **you** . . . and to others!

(Have your students consider the cartoon strip at the top of page 63, Student's Training Manual.)

How did this guy break the frozen atmosphere? By **"forcing"** a smile toward the two girls. This made them feel accepted, so they sent a smile back to him. Their smiles made him feel accepted, also! The result? **Everyone relaxed!**

Remember, when there is tension, a **forced action** will cause a **natural reaction,** resulting in **relaxation!** Try it this week! Put it to the test! You'll find it works!

And once you've loosened your lips with a smile, you'll find it's easier to speak. (If you don't know how to begin, review the rules of conversation given in your Training Manuals.)

PRINCIPLE NO. 3:

WHEN YOU FEEL LIKE EVERY EYE IS ON YOU ... TAKE COMMAND OF YOUR HANDS!

(Call attention to the cartoon character who is "all hands.")

Have you ever felt like this fellow? He's been hit with "hand hysteria"! He's certain that everyone is looking at his hands. When you feel that you're "all hands," what should you do? Should you sit on them? Shove them in your pockets? Start cracking your knuckles?

No, instead try this: Put your hands behind your back. Squeeze them into tight fists, then release them quickly letting your fingers fall loose and relaxed. *(Have your students practice this. See illustration, page 63, Student's Training Manual.)*

But now you ask, "Where should I put my hands?" Here's the simple answer: Once you've relaxed them, **forget about them!** They'll take care of themselves — **naturally!**

PRINCIPAL NO. 4:

WHEN YOU'RE FEELING FIDGETY ... DON'T GRAB A CIGARETTE! (IT'S A "NON-SOLUTION.")

Some fellows try to relieve their nervous hands by shoving a cigarette in their mouth and grabbing it out again! What are these fellows really doing? They're using their hands to tie ropes around themselves! With every puff, unseen cords are tightening around them, and these unseen cords are already leaving their marks on their bodies.

A Better Solution:

Many non-smoking business men who must spend hours around conference tables have found a better solution. They satisfy their desire for hand activity by handling some object such as a key case, pocket knife or wrist watch. Using a wrist watch as an example, this is what they might do:

(Teacher, demonstrate this for your students.)

They slip off their watch . . . look at its face . . . dangle it casually between their fingers . . . then lay it down. When they feel the urge, they pick it up again . . . stretch the band between their fingers . . . or rub the glass as though to polish it. Their movements are casual . . . slow . . . requiring no thought as they continue to listen and take part in the conversation.

"But," you say, "if everyone's smoking but me, I feel like a **baby!** And they seem **big and manly!**"

Who is really the baby?   Who is really the manly one?

Ask yourself this: Isn't the guy who can't get along without a "pacifier" in his mouth really **the baby?** And isn't the one who refuses to follow the crowd, but instead decides for himself what he'll do with his body, really **the manly one?**

Call attention to the illustration of the smokers seated around the table (page 63, Student's Training Manual). Ask your students this question:

Of the four fellows sitting around the table, which one is truly "in command" of himself?

PRINCIPLE NO. 5:

WHEN YOU'RE TRAPPED BY FEAR AND SELF-CONCERN . . . SHOW LOVE TO THE OTHER PERSON

Much self-consciousness is caused by fears. Let's look at the first section of our cartoon strip, bottom of page 63. *(Read aloud.)*

> "Hmmm . . . wonder what he thinks of me . . . Will he reject me? I'm afraid he thinks I'm stupid! Guess I really am!"

Many of us are like this fellow. We're afraid of what the other person might think! We're afraid of losing his approval! But God has provided a way to banish these fears. The next section of our cartoon shows us how. *(Read aloud.)*

> "Hold on here! God loves me . . . just like I am . . . This guy's not perfect either . . . and he knows it, too! God's given me his love . . . so I'll pass it on to this guy!"

When you find yourself becoming fearful around another person, tell yourself the same three things this fellow told himself.

First: God loves me — just like I am!

This will get your eyes off "self" and on to **God!**

Secondly: This guy's not perfect either . . . and he knows it, too!

Remind yourself that the other fellow has fears, too! "That cocky fellow?"   Yes — that   cocky   fellow — no matter how self-confident he may appear! Psychiatrists tell us that the fellow who swaggers the loudest is often the one with the most fears. In his blustering, he's simply trying to "out-shout" his feelings of inadequacy.

Thirdly: God's given me his love . . . so I'll pass it on to this guy!

What will be the result? Let's look at the last section of our cartoon. *(Read aloud.)*

"Hmmm . . . that's funny! He doesn't scare me any more! He looks different now! He's just another human being like me who needs to feel that people like him, too!"

When you tell yourself these three things, you'll see the other person in a new light. You'll feel love and compassion toward him. You'll realize he's simply another guy with needs — like you! And as you let God's love flow through you to him, he'll sense your spirit of love — and he'll respond to it!

How can you be sure he'll respond? Because all the world responds to love — because all the world desperately **needs** love! If this weren't true, why does God urge us to "dish it out" **unsparingly** to everyone!

"Love your neighbor," he tells us. "Love your enemy . . . love your brother . . . love one another!"

God knows that in filling the **other** person's need, we'll find our **own** need fulfilled also! Try it! You'll see it works!

Have your students complete the scripture verse given in their Training Manuals at the bottom of page 63. "Perfect love casts out fear" (1 John 4:18).

PRINCIPLE NO. 6:

WHEN YOU FEEL LIKE A MISFIT . . . TAKE ACTION!
(Page 64, Student's Training Manual)

Sometimes it's necessary to make an effort to keep from feeling like a misfit! Our Training Manuals give us four suggestions to follows.

1. Develop social skills. Learn to play their games.

If you find yourself sitting on the sidelines watching others have fun, take steps to change the picture! If bowling parties are in style, learn to bowl! (You may like it!) If folk songs are the "in" thing, give it a try! (You may become an asset to your group.) The greater number of social skills you possess, the more easily you'll fit in with a group.

2. Pay attention to what others are wearing and try to dress similarly.

You might ask, "How can I know what others will wear?"

When you are invited, simply inquire "What will it be? School clothes or Sunday clothes?"

If you find yourself completely in the dark, stay in the middle of the road. If you should make a wrong guess and turn up at the party wearing the wrong thing, don't let it ruin your fun (and everyone else's). When others see that you're not concerned about your "outer covering," they'll forget it too!

3. Cooperate! Volunteer your help! Get into the action!

Working with others will help you feel like one of the team. Don't hang back! When help is needed to hang decorations, **volunteer!** When someone is needed to bring equipment, **offer your help!** Get into the action! Do telephoning . . . make posters . . . arrange transportation. Onlookers are misfits; participants are not! **Remember,** "A man that hath friends must show himself friendly" (Prov. 18:24). This means that your actions must demonstrate that you are open to friendship.

4. Remember people's names — and use them!

Nothing is more pleasing to a person's ears than the sound of his own name! Here are some tips to help you remember a new name:

- Keep a notebook in your pocket and when you have an opportunity, enter the new name in your notebook as a reminder.
- Repeat the name several times during the conversation.
- Find a word-association to link with the new name. (For example, if you meet Carol Smith at a Christmas social, remember her name by associating it with a "Christmas Carol.")

PRINCIPLE NO. 7:

WHEN OTHERS OVERWHELM YOU ... REMEMBER THAT YOU'RE NOT INFERIOR — ONLY DIFFERENT!

Some teenagers feel overshadowed by another person's personality, appearance or achievements. They shrink into a shell — overcome by feelings of inferiority.

Has this ever happened to you? If so, remember this: Failing to measure up to **another person's** capabilities does not make you an inferior person. You become inferior only by failing to live up to **your own** God-given capabilities — **not someone else's.**

You have your own special gifts.

If God didn't give you long arms and legs, why feel inferior to the star basketball player? You have gifts that he may not have. The star basketball player may not be able to speak like you ... or repair cars ... or grow vegetables ... or make others feel important by being a good listener.

Furthermore, God may have a different timetable for the use of your gifts. Some talents require years of preparation. Whereas the star player appears in the limelight now (and possibly for the next few years) your acclaim may come later — **and last longer!**

Have your students read the scripture verses given in their Training Manuals.

PRINCIPLE NO. 8:

IF YOU WANT SOCIAL SUCCESS ... DON'T LOOK FOR IT IN A BOTTLE! (GRABBING A DRINK IS A "NON-SOLUTION.")

Some fellows are afraid to face a social gathering without grabbing a drink or two to bolster their confidence. But this is simply a cop-out for cowards and for those who care nothing about developing their social skills. If a guy depends upon the **false** confidence liquor gives, he'll never build **true** social confidence. Each time he says, "I need a drink," he is admitting that he can't make it on his own.

"But," you may say, "won't a drink or two make me more jovial and sociable? Won't it help me to be more talkative and free around others?"

A loose tongue can be harmful.

Drinking **does** make a person more talkative, but in the **wrong** way! It loosens his tongue by removing the inhibitions that normally guard his words. The Bible says that the tongue is an unruly member harder to control than wild animals. (See Jas. 3:2-8.) Why make the problem worse?

> **The man in demand is the man in command**
> **Of that unruly member — his tongue:**
> **For a mouth that is loose**
> **Makes an excellent noose,**
> **With his very own words, he is hung!**

Call attention to the cartoon (bottom of page 64, Student's Training Manual) which shows a fellow being "hung" by his words. Read the scripture verses.

Drinking produces childish behavior — not joyousness.

The person who drinks appears unusually jovial merely because he's taken a step backward toward childishness. The drinker's seeming joviality is the sugar-coating Satan places on his poison pill. The sweet outer layer of the pill dissolves rapidly, and when it's too late, the partaker finds he has swallowed something harmful and bitter "that biteth like a serpent and stingeth like an adder." (See Prov. 23:32.)

If you stay with ginger ale, you'll not miss out on any true enjoyment. The only thing you'll miss will be the "woe" and "sorrow" the Bible says will come to those who "tarry long at the wine." (See Prov. 23:29, 30.)

"But," you ask, "won't drinking help make me a social success like the men shown in the liquor ads?"

Is this the way to social success?

Is this the kind of behavior that will make your hostess like you? Or **anyone else, for that matter?**

- To shoot off your mouth?
- To become noisy and reckless?
- To become touchy and ready to fight?
- To become foolish and silly — laughing uncontrollably?
- To stumble over furniture and spill food?
- To become suddenly nauseated and be forced to vomit?
- To become insulting and rude, abandoning courtesy and manners?
- To draw attention to yourself by inappropriate behavior?
- To embarrass the girl you brought to the party by becoming gushy and over-affectionate?
- To endanger her life when you drive her home from the party, and thus betray the trust her parents placed in you?

"But," you say, "the kids make it tough for anyone to refuse a drink. They even try to **force** it on you! How can you make them understand you don't want one?"

How to refuse a drink:

Be plain and clear from the start! Let them see that you expect them to respect your decision. And **don't** apologize! (Would you feel that you had to apologize for not accepting a glass of polluted water?)

Ask yourself this question:

If these guys were drinking lemonade, would they try to force me to drink lemonade with them?

Of course, not! Then why do they become upset if you decline a beer? Because your refusal to go along with them is a silent rebuke, and they desperately need your approval. Secretly they wish they had your backbone. Secretly they admire you. The wise course is to **keep** their admiration!

Following the wrong crowd can lead down the wrong path!

If you repeatedly find that you're the only one in your crowd refusing to drink, look for another crowd!

"But," you may ask, "what harm is there in running with a certain crowd if you don't **do** the things they do?"

The Bible says, "Evil companions corrupt good morals" (1 Cor. 15:33). Teenagers who have gotten into trouble will tell you this is true.

"I never dreamed I'd do the things I did!" they say. "When I was with the gang, I did things I'd never do alone!"

If you repeatedly feel uneasy with a certain group, consider this a warning to get back into God's crowd. You're sure to feel more at home there, because you're "just another member of the family" — **God's family!**

PRINCIPLE NO. 9:

WHEN GUILT CREEPS IN . . . DEAL WITH IT GOD'S WAY!
(Page 65, Student's Training Manual)

Some of you may be thinking, "Yeah, but I've already gotten into the wrong crowd, and I've done things I'm ashamed of. Sometimes it's hard to look others in the eye. How can I get rid of this guilty conscience?"

Nothing will ruin your happiness — or your personality — more quickly than a guilty conscience. If you want to feel relaxed around others, do nothing that you must later hide from others.

If you've already done things that make you feel guilty, deal with them God's way. Confess them and accept God's forgiveness. Forgive yourself, too! Satan (who is the "accuser of the brethren") may try to taunt you with your sin. But refuse to let him drag up the past. Let memories of past misdeeds serve only to remind you of God's forgiveness and to make you more careful to avoid the wrong path in the future.

Every member of the human race has felt the pangs of guilt. Jesus Christ was the only one who never had reason to feel shame. That's why he is the only one qualified to help us.

Have your students quietly consider the scriptures on page 65 of their Training Manuals which describe Christ's work on the cross. Call attention to the cartoon strip. Point out that God not only forgives — but also forgets!

PRINCIPLE NO. 10:

WHEN YOU NEED COURAGE TO FACE PROBLEMS... TAP IN ON JESUS' STRENGTH AND POWER!

Don't wait until you're faced with a jungle full of lions and tigers to learn to holler, "Jesus, HELP ME!" Start learning now to deal with your everyday social fears by seeking his strength.

> Do you sometimes shake in your boots?
> Do you ever feel timid as a mouse?
> Do you sometimes feel completely helpless?
> Do you fear you'll be teased or ridiculed?
> Are you afraid you can't possibly succeed?

Learn the verses given in your Training Manuals. When you feel overwhelmed, repeat them to yourself. You'll see results!

SIX SELF-CONSCIOUS FELLOWS WHO NEED HELP
(Pages 66-67 Student's Training Manual)

On pages 66 and 67 in our Training Manuals we find six self-conscious fellows who need help. First, consider their problems. Then write a few words of advice for each one. Base your advice on the instruction you have just received.

When your students have completed this assignment, ask several to read their answers. Appropriate answers are as follows:

Petrified Pete: Straighten up and smile! Take command of your hands!

Fidgety Freddie: Get rid of those fidgety hands by handling your watch or knife. Sit up straight, and you'll feel more confident! Don't forget that **you** are the "manly one" — the one in command of himself — **not** the smokers!

Howard the Coward: Realize you've chosen a dangerous "non-solution" which will keep you from developing **true** social confidence and social skills.

Dudley the Dud: Make an effort to "fit in"! Get involved in the activities! Learn some social skills!

Over-spruced Bruce: Try to discover ahead of time what others will be wearing. If you "goof," forget it and have a good time anyway!

Over-awed Claude: Don't feel like a "nobody"! You are not inferior — only different! You have your special abilities, too!

Of course, every fellow in every situation of life needs to let Jesus give him confidence and strength!

Prayer:

Father God, sometimes we feel awkward. We worry about the impression we're making. We get our eyes on "self" and we freeze up!

Deliver us from our fears so we can be natural and relaxed around others. Help us to live such clean lives that we'll have no reason to hide behind masks. But if we do wrong, may we confess the wrong to you; and having experienced your forgiving love, may we love others — unconditionally — just as you love us, through Jesus Christ, Your Son. Amen.

Memory Question No. 11: Of what truth should we remind ourselves when we need confidence and courage to face difficult situations?

Answer: "I can do all things through Christ which strengtheneth me" (Phil 4:13).

PREVENTING GROOMING DISORDERS

(Pages 68 — 74, Student's Training Manual)

YOU WILL NEED: Examples of various types of closet accessories and hangers. Sport jacket, pants and shirt for use in suggested demonstration, page 184.

To open your session, relate the following story to your class:

SHORTSIGHTED TED

Ted was excited! In a few minutes he'd be picking up Linda to take her to the Teen Rally. For several weeks he'd been telling her about God and urging her to come to church with him. Finally she had consented.

This was his important night — and he wanted the car to look sharp! That's why he'd been scrubbing and polishing all afternoon. Now it was ready for the finishing touches.

With swift, vigorous strokes, Ted brushed the dust from the bucket seats. He grabbed the trash basket and emptied it. Now . . . with one last swipe across the dashboard the job was done!

Ted stepped back to admire his work. Yep! The car sure looked snappy — just like he wanted it to! Dashing into the house, he grabbed his Bible and ran out again, whistling as he went.

Ted was right on one count — girls **are** impressed with cleanliness! But shortsighted Ted didn't carry his cleanliness routine far enough. Although Linda was transported to the rally in a spotless car, she had to sit beside a tousle-headed boy with ripped shirt, grimy pants and dirty fingernails. Furthermore, she had to endure an unpleasant odor of perspiration which lingered about him from his hard work.

Linda's thoughts as they drove to the rally went something like this: **"If this Jesus-Person has cleaned Ted up on the inside like he says, you'd think some of it would show through to the outside, too!"**

WAS LINDA'S THINKING RIGHT?

Is there a connection between Godliness and cleanliness?

Let your students express their ideas. Then explain as follows:

Linda's thinking was right. Cleanliness is associated with Godliness — and for a good reason! When a person surrenders himself totally to Jesus Christ, his body is included in the transaction. And because his body has become the Lord's property, it must be kept clean.

DISRESPECT TO THE MAKER

Jim's mother labored hard for many weeks to make a beautiful quilt for her son. Soon afterward she died. Because the quilt was something his mother had made especially for him, Jim cherished it greatly.

One day, upon returning from a hike in the woods, Jim brought his pal into his bedroom to unload their gear. Exhausted, Jim's pal flopped down on the bed, brushing his muddy boots against the quilt and snagging it with the sharp eyelet hooks.

"Watch out!" Jim cried. "Look what you're doing to my quilt!" His pal looked up in surprise.

"Sorry," he said, "but why get so excited?   It's just an old quilt!"

After a long pause Jim replied in a low voice. "It may be 'just an old quilt' to you . . . but I'll have you know my mother made that!"

Immediately Jim's pal understood: To show disrespect to the quilt was to show disrespect to the one who had made it.

WHAT ABOUT OUR BODIES?

When we show disrespect to our bodies, are we showing disrespect to the one who made them? David, the Psalmist, deeply appreciated the body God gave him. He wrote:

"I will praise thee; for I am fearfully and wonderfully made: marvelous are thy works" (Ps. 139:14).

Will a wrong attitude toward God produce a wrong attitude toward the body?

Certainly a faulty perspective of God will create an improper attitude toward the body he created for us. Take the savage, for example. Because his mind was darkened with fear and superstition, he cut his body, deformed his members, marked and tatooed his skin in hideous fashion. The derelict on skid row who has renounced God's laws in his heart also renounces cleanliness in his body — and decent grooming as well!

John Wesley expressed the connection this way: "Cleanliness is indeed next to Godliness." If God has made us clean **inside,** it behooves us to keep clean **outside** — just as Linda reasoned!

"ON-THE-SPOT" GROOMING CHECK

How are you caring for the body God gave you? The "On-the-Spot" Grooming Check in your Training Manuals (page 68) will show you where you stand.

Have your students complete the quiz. Note the score chart instructions on page 69.

WHAT DID YOUR GROOMING CHECK REVEAL?

Are you less than perfectly groomed? If so, you're not alone! Most fellows have grooming problems. But the ones who make no attempt to correct them are the losers! Poor grooming works against these fellows in every area of their lives — in their relationships with their teachers, their girl friends, their neighbors, their bosses — and even with their families. On the other hand, there's much to be gained by learning the principles of good grooming.

GOOD GROOMING BEGINS WITH CLEANLINESS

To be well-groomed, you must be clean all over. The easiest way to achieve this is to take a bath! Nothing makes you look better than an old-fashioned soap-and-water scrubbing!

A bath makes an important impact upon your senses, too. Stop and think. What can compare with the "I-can-conquer-the-world" feeling that envelops you as you step out of your bath? You not only **look** clean, but you also **feel** clean! You look and feel like a young man who deserves the **best!** Of course, you'll put on clean clothes! Of course, you'll make sure they're in order! Your bath has given you more than a clean body — it's also given you the self-respect that inspires further good grooming.

WARNING! SKIP YOUR BATH AT YOUR OWN RISK!
(Page 70, Student's Training Manual)

Start the day with a bath — and good grooming follows! Skip your bath and the entire process goes into reverse gear — like this: Shirt wrinkled? . . . "It'll pass!" Button missing? . . . "I'll grab a pin!" Pants grubby? . . . "No one'll notice!"

One neglect leads to another. Our Training Manuals show us the "serious retrograde action" that can take place when a fellow skips his bath.

Call your students' attention to the downward steps and final outcome of the cartoon character depicted on page 70, Student's Training Manual.

WHEN AND HOW SHALL I BATHE?

"Shall I bathe in the morning or in the evening?"

It doesn't matter, as long as you bathe **regularly!** Some boys feel that a morning bath envigorates them for the day, while others prefer to bathe at bedtime.

"Shall I tub-bathe or shower?"

"By all means, shower! A hot tub bath could be sexually stimulating — and this you'll want to avoid.

To begin your shower, flush away the surface dirt with a quick rinse-off. Then, starting at your head and working down to your toes, give yourself a total lathering all over. Finish with a cool rinse.

When you step out of your bath, grab a man-sized towel and start rubbing — **vigorously!** A brisk rub-down peps up your circulation. As a precaution against athlete's feet, dry carefully between your toes. This is a good time to trim those toenails, too. To avoid ingrown toenails, cut your nails straight across.

NOW REACH FOR A DEODORANT!

"A deodorant! But **why?**" you demand. "**I just had a bath!**"

Reasonable as your objection may sound, a bath is no insurance that you'll remain odorless all day. **What happens?**

- Your classroom is warm ... the test is difficult ... **you perspire!**
- The cafeteria is jammed ... the air is humid ... **you perspire!**
- The last bell has rung ... you rush up the stairs ... **you perspire!**

With perspiration comes offensive body odors. Underarm odors are particularly disagreeable, and underarm moisture rings damage your clothing.

To avoid this unpleasantness, make regular use of a deodorant or antiperspirant. (A deodorant stops underarm odor; an antiperspirant also stops underarm odor but at the same time restricts the flow of perspiration.)

Choose the one best suited to your needs; then use it regularly in cool weather as well as warm — and whether you think you need it or not! Don't wait until your nose tells you you're offending. Your nose can fail you! You can become so gradually accustomed to your own body-odor that you're not aware of it. But that doesn't mean that others are not aware of it — and much annoyed by it!

"C.O." (CLOTHING ODOR)

Some boys who bathe regularly and use a deodorant daily still carry an obnoxious odor about them. They don't have "B.O." (body odor); instead they have "C.O." (clothing odor). These boys "put on" an odor when they put on their clothes!

Take "Smelly Sam," for instance. Sam always smells like a blend of mothballs, garlic and mildew. Why? Because these odors permeate the apartment building where Sam lives, and his clothes (especially his sweaters and woolens) absorb the odors. What's the answer to "Smelly Sam's" problem? Besides following a regular cleaning schedule, he needs to air his clothes by an open window at night. If he does this, he'll soon lose his nickname.

"S.S." (SMELLY SHOES)

Some boys need to place another item beside their window at night. These are the ones who have "S.S." (smelly shoes). Yes, shoes need airing, too!

When you exercise heavily, your feet perspire. When your feet perspire, you develop "soggy socks," and soggy socks soon produce smelly shoes. When this happens, wash your feet, sprinkle them with foot powder and put on clean, dry socks and shoes. Sprinkle foot powder inside your shoes, too.

Sneakers are usually the worst offenders. Fortunately they can be washed. Don't wait too long to do it.

Instead of wearing one pair of shoes steadily, it's a good idea to alternate between several pairs.

"B.B." (BAD BREATH)

If your breath smells, no one wants to be near you. If "B.B." (bad breath) is your problem, follow these tips:

First, brush your teeth twice a day to rout out food particles. (Brush with an up-and-down stroke.)

Second, keep your teeth free of decay with regular dental check-ups.

Third, use a hygienic mouth wash. (A salt water gargle works well.)

Fourth, carry breath purifiers for those times when you may need them.

How will you know when you need a breath purifier? If you've been eating odorous foods such as garlic, you're sure to need one. If you notice a bad taste in your mouth, you should take this as a warning. When in doubt, give yourself a breath test.

Cup your hands between your mouth and nose. Exhale — then breathe in. Pay attention to even the slightest odor. It may be more noticeable to others. *(See illustration at bottom of page 70 in Training Manual.)*

WATCH OUT FOR THESE "POPULARITY POISONS"!

Call attention to the cartoon depicting the girl's reaction to the fellow's "popularity-poisons." Have your students complete the chart beneath the cartoon by identifying the "popularity poisons" and their "antidotes."

Correct answers are as follows:

B.O. — Body Odor   — Antidotes (3) and (6).

S.S. — Smelly Shoes   — Antidotes (1), (4), (7), and (8).

B.B. — Bad Breath   — Antidotes (2), (5), and (9).

C.O. — Clothing Odor — Antidotes (1) and (10).

USE YOUR EYES TO EXAMINE YOUR CLOTHES

The girl sitting on the sofa has a nose that can be offended. But that's not all! She has eyes that can be offended also!

Are you visually offensive? How can you make sure you're "easy-to-look-at"? By using **your** eyes — just like the girl uses **hers!**

Before you put on your clothes, give each article a thorough "top-sergeant" inspection. Take your shirt, for example. Are the cuffs dingy? Flatten them out so you can examine the inside edges. Are dirt and food spots sprinkled down the front? Hold your shirt at eye-level so you can look squarely at it. Is the neckline soiled? Unfold the collar out flat for inspection. But perhaps you still can't decide whether your shirt is clean or dirty. When you're "on the fence," lean toward the side of cleanliness.

A boy called downstairs to his mother, "Mom, tell me if this shirt is clean!"

The answer came back instantly, "No, it's **not!**"

"But Mom," the boy hollered back, "how can you tell from down there?"

"Simple!" she answered. "If you have to **ask** if it's clean — it's **not!**"

TAKE A "MIRROR CHECK"
(Page 71, Student's Training Manual)

You've checked over your clothes. You've found them clean. You've put them on, and you're heading toward the door. **Hold on there!** Have you given yourself a "mirror check?"

It's not enough that your clothes appear orderly hanging on their hangers. They must also appear orderly **"hanging on you"!**

Have your students list "Messy Mertyn's grooming disorders (page 71, Student's Training Manual).

Correct answers are as follows:

1. T-Shirt on backward, and label protruding.
2. Buttons missing or not fastened.
3. Shirt half in and half out.
4. Zipper unfastened.
5. Belt not threaded through loops.
6. Pants leg rolled up.
7. Sock sagging around ankle.
8. Shoelaces untied and frazzled.
9. Pants wrinkled and in need of pressing.

TAKE A CLOSET CHECK!
(Page 71, Student's Training Manual)

Is your closet a mess?

When your closet's messy, your clothes will look messy too! Pants dumped in a heap on the closet floor look crumpled. Jackets dangling lopsided on hangers look misshapen. Shirts jammed together look crushed. And if your clothes look disorderly — so will you! Your closet is meant to serve you. But some boys receive no benefits from their closets at all.

Take "Donald the Draper," for instance:

Donald drapes his clothes on everything! He'll hang clothes on any object in his room — so long as it's not a clothes hanger. Step into his bedroom and you'll have a hard time finding his furniture. The chairs, lamps and bed are hidden from view — completely covered with his clothes. When you want to leave his room, you're faced with another problem. His door knobs are covered, too! If by chance you exit into a dark, oblong enclosure that appears to be a short, dead-end hall — **back out!** You've wandered into his empty closet by mistake!

Next, there's "One-Hook Harry:"

When Harry's Mom looks at his closet, she shakes her head and says kindly, "Well . . . poor Harry . . . he **tries!**"

Take one look at his closet and you'll see what she means. Harry does try **hard!** He tries to hang all his clothes on **one hook** — and you'll have to agree, **that is hard!**

And then there's "Steve-the Slinger:"

His clothes never get near the closet at all! His mother says, "He's never hung up a garment in his life. He just **slings 'em,** and wherever they land — **that's it!** Except for his pants, of course. They stay right where he steps out of them at night!"

These three fellows obviously haven't learned to make use of their closets. Have you?

Refer your students to the 2 closets illustrated in their Training Manuals (page 71). Ask your students this question: Which closet most nearly resembles your own? Would your Mom agree?

HOW TO TAKE COMMAND OF YOUR CLOSET

Once you've taken command of your closet, your life will be easier and your appearance will be sharper! Here's how you "take command:"

First — Clean your closet.

Remove any clutter that belongs in your attic or garage.

Second — Organize your clothes.

Hang all your pants together, your shirts together, etc. Out of season items belong toward the back. Shoes belong in a shoe rack, belts on a belt rack, and ties on a tie rack.

Third — Store your clothes properly.

Close the button openings or zippers if this is necessary to hold your clothes in shape. Brush off any dandruff, lint or dog hairs. Empty overloaded pockets.

Fourth — Hang your clothes properly.

Use the correct type of hanger. Don't hang loose-weave, stretchy garments on closet hooks (or door knobs either). The weight of the article will produce an unsightly bulge at the point of support.

Call attention to illustration of "door knob bulge" (bottom of page 71, Student's Training Manual).

CAN YOU PASS THE "CLOTHES HANGER TEST"?
(Page 72, Student's Training Manual)

Have your students take the "Clothes Hanger Test" in their Training Manuals. Correct answers are as follows:

Sport Jacket — Hanger No. 2
Shirt — Hanger No. 1
Pants — Hanger No. 4 or 5
Shorts — Hanger No. 4
Dress Suit — Hanger No. 3 or 5

CLOTHES HANGING DEMONSTRATION

You may want to bring several articles of clothing to class to provide the following visual demonstration for your students.

Pants or Shorts

Show the students how to maintain the identical crease-line by (1) gripping the cuff or bottoms; (2) aligning them evenly so that the crease-line falls into place; and (3) maintaining the correct fold lines as they are clamped into the hanger.

Note: Pants may also be folded over a hanger-bar. Clamp hangers are preferable, however, because they allow the pants to hang full length. The full weight of the pants helps to remove wrinkles and prolong the crease.

Bring an example of pants which have hung folded for several days over a wire hanger. Point out the unsightly horizontal creases that have developed on the pants legs.

Jackets and Coats

First, hang a jacket on a shaped hanger to show the students how the curve of the hanger helps maintain the natural shape of the collar and curve of the shoulder line.

Next, hang the same jacket on a wire hanger. Call attention to the pronounced wrinkle that develops at the collar and shoulders as well as the sags and folds that appear in the body of the jacket.

Shirts

Demonstrate the wrong way to hang a shirt (dangling lopsided, etc.) and the right way (evenly balanced on hanger with shoulders centered over hanger, top button fastened, etc.).

NEVER HANG THESE IN YOUR CLOSET

Refer students to Training Manuals. Have them complete the 3 statements by describing the items which should not be hung in their closets.

Correct answers are as follows:

1. Garments that are rain-dampened.
2. Garments that are ripped, torn, damaged or in need of repair.
3. Garments that are muddy, grease-stained, soiled, or in need of cleaning or laundering before the next wearing.

"DELAYED-ACTION DAN"

Don't be a "delayed-action Dan"! When Dan tears his Sunday jacket, he doesn't bother to mention it. When he rips the seat of his dress pants, he remains mum. Quietly he puts his "problems" to rest in his closet — out of sight, out of mind throughout the entire week. Then, five minutes before church — he explodes, **"Mom!!! You didn't fix my pants!!! I have no jacket to wear!!! I can't go!"**

It's too late for Dan to holler now. He should have used his vocal chords earlier, and he should not have hung these "unwearables" in his closet.

TAKE PREVENTATIVE ACTION NOW

"A stitch in time saves nine." The proverb is true; preventative action does pay!

When you see your stitching coming loose, take care of it **now!** Why wait until the seam pops wide open in class?

When you find a rip or tear, mention it **now!** Why wait until the edges fray and the hole gets so big it can't be mended successfully?

When you see a button dangling on one thread, pull it off and sew it on **now!** (Yes, men often sew on buttons!) Why wait until it drops off and becomes lost? Some buttons are hard to match, and you may have to replace 9 instead of one — just as the proverb warns! Smart guys avoid big problems later by caring for small problems **now!**

SHOES NEED CARE AND REPAIR

Regular shoe care helps your shoes last longer and look better. Keep a shoe brush handy in your closet for a daily dust-off and a weekly shine.

When you come in from the rain, don't set your sopping shoes next to direct heat. Quick drying shrinks shoes stiff and hard. Dry them slowly in a cool place. Then work shoe grease into the leather until it becomes soft and pliable again.

Wear socks with shoes, of course — not only to look well-groomed but also to protect your feet from friction against the inside of your shoes.

If you have athlete's feet, avoid wool socks or tightly woven fabrics such as nylon. Doctors recommend white cotton socks for athlete's feet.

DON'T LET YOUR HANDS BECOME A HANDICAP!
Hands need grooming, too!

Boys' hands? Yes! Have you ever considered how often your hands come into the spotlight? Stop and think.

1. You gesture and motion with your hands.
2. You greet others by shaking hands with them.
3. You pass and receive objects with your hands.
4. You express your emotions with your hands.
5. Your hands play a leading role when you eat.

Call attention to illustrations in Training Manual, bottom of page 72.

It's unrealistic to think no one will notice your long, dirty fingernails or your grimy knuckles. **Girls will!** As we see from this illustration, girls are often repulsed by such sights. If you want to offer that special girl the "hand of friendship," make sure it's a well-groomed one!

Of course, hands are bound to get dirty now and then, but why let them stay that way? If you do, your hands are sure to become a handicap!

Have your students read from their Training Manuals the suggestions given under the headings, "Keep Your Hands Well-Groomed" and "Keep Your Nails Properly Trimmed."

DON'T LET YOUR GROOMING "GO UP IN SMOKE"!
(Page 73, Student's Training Manual)

Young fellows who value their masculine appeal at all (or who value themselves at all) rule out cigarettes. Our Training Manuals (page 73) list three reasons why. Do these reasons make sense? You be the judge!

REASON NO. 1
Ask a student to read aloud the "warning from the Surgeon General."

REASON NO. 2
Ask a student to read aloud the "warning from God's Word." Have your students complete the scripture reference (1 Cor. 3:17) by filling in the missing words.

REASON NO. 3

Select two students to read the spoken parts in the dialogue between the boy and the girl in the cartoon.

NOW IS THE TIME TO THINK OF YOUR FUTURE

One question the boy in the cartoon strip didn't bother to ask the girl is this: "Will you and your children like it someday when you have to bury your husband 17 years too soon?"

The girl is still too young to relate to the reality of the future (even though it comes very quickly). But now is the time for you to think about your future, for the tobacco habit starts with the first cigarette.

Don't be fooled by those who boast, "I can stop smoking any time I please!" Winston Churchill rightly said, "Will-power is a quality that every person possesses up to the day he decides to give up smoking."

"INNER GROOMING"

Outward grooming without "inner grooming" doesn't count for much.

Earlier you heard the story of "shortsighted Ted" who cleaned his car — but not himself — before his date with Linda.

When Linda rode with Ted to the Teen Rally, you recall, she was displeased with his appearance — naturally! Ted made a poor impression on her — and this was still fresh in her mind when she had a date the following Saturday night with a fellow named Ralph.

When Linda stepped into Ralph's car that evening, her first impression was a good one. **"Now here's a nice-looking guy!"** she thought. "His hair's brushed, his nails are clean, he's polished and scrubbed ... he even smells good — like refreshing woodsy cologne!"

Then Linda's thoughts wandered back to her date with Ted the week before. "Too bad Ted doesn't take better care of himself," she thought.

Settling back in her cushioned seat, Linda anticipated a "fun evening" with a nice guy! At this point, however, her expectations were based solely on Ralph's outer appearance.

Two hours later, Linda stomped up the stairs to her house, her face flushed with anger, her hair a mess, her blouse ripped, and the sound of Ralph's filthy jokes still grating on her ears.

Why was she angry? Because Ralph had tried to make a plaything of her . . . because he hadn't treated her with respect! His fine appearance didn't count for much now. In Linda's eyes, his well-groomed hair simply covered a contaminated mind. His spotless shirt simply hid a soiled heart.

Jesus had strong words for such men. He said, "You're like cups and platters that are shining clean on the outside but filthy dirty on the inside! You're like tombs that hold dead-men's bones — outwardly beautiful and white, but inwardly foul and unclean!"

Was Jesus inferring that their outer condition didn't matter? Not at all! He was simply telling them that their priorities were mixed up. They were careful to maintain outward appearances but neglected the inner cleanliness of their souls!

Jesus reminded them that the same God who made their bodies made their souls also. "Cleanse first that which is within," he told them, "so that the outside may be clean also." (See Matt. 23:26).

The fellow who cares nothing about how he looks inside may look good to others at first sight — but not for long. **Ralph didn't!**

YOUR DAILY "SOUL GROOMING"
(Page 74, Student's Training Manual)

How do you look to God? The Bible tells us that nothing is hidden from him. "All things are naked and opened unto the eyes of him with whom we have to do" (Heb. 4:13).

Call attention to the two illustrations on page 74 of the Training Manual. Read aloud the scripture verses above the first illustration only at this time.

SILENT PRAYER:

Following the reading of the scripture verses, ask the students to bow their heads and silently ask God to show them anything in their lives that is displeasing to him.

After a few moments of silence and while students' heads are still bowed, quietly read the scripture verses above the second illustration.

Call your students' attention to the poem, "Good Morning, Lord!" which describes a fellow's thoughts as he considers how he looks to God.

DAILY "CHECK-UP"

Encourage your students to cut out the Daily "Check-Up" list and place it on their bedroom mirror as a daily reminder to consider "how they look to God" — as well as "how they look to man."

Memory Question No. 12: In what way does God view us differently from man?

Answer: "The Lord seeth not as man seeth; for man looketh on the outward appearance, but the Lord looketh on the heart" (1 Sam. 16:7).

PERFECTING YOUR MANNERS

(Pages 75 — 79, Student's Training Manual)

PRIOR TO CLASS: Determine whether or not you will invite someone to assist you as a "hostess" for this session. Consider having a "demonstration and practice table" as described on page 203.

FOLLOW THE GOLDEN RULE

Any game you play with others must be played by the rules. Your social life involves others. Therefore it must be played by the rules too! The "golden rule" of good manners is the Golden Rule of the scriptures: "Therefore all things whatsoever ye would that men should do to you, do ye even so to them" (Matt. 7:12).

AVOID THE THINGS YOU DISLIKE IN OTHERS

A wise man was once asked, "From whom did you learn manners?" He answered, **"From the unmannerly!"** The things which annoyed him in others, he avoided doing himself.

Do you enjoy eating with someone who gulps his food? Chews with his mouth open? Lets food drool down his lips? Of course not! Therefore, to follow the golden rule, you will want to eat quietly, chew with your mouth closed and use your napkin frequently. Make this your rule: "Eat as neatly for **others** as you would want them to do for **you!"**

MANNERS MUST BE PRACTICED REGULARLY

You might ask, "Is it all right to eat any way I please when I'm alone?" You **can** — but if you're smart, you **won't!** Why not? Because in order for your table manners to become an ingrained pattern in your life, they must be practiced consistently. Only when your table manners become a **natural** thing, will you be able to **"act natural"** when eating with others. If you're constantly on guard lest you slip back into the sloppy habits you practice at home, you'll feel tense and uncomfortable. Others will feel uncomfortable around you likewise. You'll make poor table company. You may not be invited back again!

DON'T REBEL AGAINST THE RULES

Perhaps you are thinking: "Why should I have to follow some ancient rules written down in some old etiquette book — especially when some of the rules don't make sense?"

Let's look at it this way: Table etiquette is simply a system of eating which has been figured out in years past through trial and error. This accumulated knowledge has been handed down to free you from the burden of figuring out fresh solutions for each new eating problem. Following the rules will make life easier for you — and for those around you, too!

THE "EATING GAME" REQUIRES TEAM WORK

Eating together at a common table, serving yourself from a common dish, passing objects from one to another is in a very real sense a team effort. Like any other game, it will progress more successfully when every player follows the rules laid down in advance.

If you make up your own rules as you go along, others won't be expecting your plays and passes. The result? Confusion, spills and awkward situations!

GOOD MANNERS MAKE SENSE

Practicing good manners, therefore, is first of all a way of showing consideration to others; and secondly, a way of operating more easily in a "team play" with others.

Good manners are not "for women only" — nor are they "for sissies only"! On the contrary, good manners are the mark of a real man! **To be truly manly, you must be mannerly!**

Three fellows are described on page 75 of our Training Manuals — The "Hostess Harasser," The "Thoughtless Dinner Guest," and "Mr. Repulsive." Let's consider the table manners of each one of these fellows.

Read the items listed beneath each of the headings. Most are self-explanatory, but you may wish to make additional comments as follows regarding some of the items mentioned:

DON'T BE A "HOSTESS HARASSER"

What should you do when you find that you're going to be late?

Most hostesses do not plan to serve dinner immediately upon their guests' arrival. However, if you see that you're going to be 15 or 20 minutes late, telephone your hostess, make a brief explanation and suggest that she not wait dinner for you.

What should you do when you enter the dining room?

First, wait for your hostess to tell you where she wants you to sit. Then as a mark of respect, remain standing until your hostess is seated. It shows respect also for a boy to remain standing until girls, women or older persons have been seated. Remember to honor your mother in this way, too.

What should you do when you find a foreign object in your food?

Keep quiet about it and proceed as normally as possible under the circumstances. Rather than drawing attention to it, and thereby embarrassing the hostess, simply bypass the object (if possible) as you are eating.

How can you keep in step with others?

Keep an eye on the other guests' plates as you are eating. Try neither to eat too slowly nor too fast. If you see that everyone else's plate is almost empty and yours is still heaped, it's time to **eat** — rather than **talk!** It is impolite to unnecessarily delay the dinner's progress.

What's wrong with leaving food uneaten?

Leaving food uneaten is not only upsetting to the hostess but is also wasteful and morally wrong in consideration of the food shortages existing in the world. **Take all you want, but eat all you take!**

DON'T BE A "THOUGHTLESS DINNER GUEST"

Read the items listed beneath this heading in the Student's Training Manual. Make comments as follows:

How do you help a girl into her seat?

Refer your students to the illustrations at the top of page 78, Student's Training Manual. This can be practiced now or during the Demonstration and Practice Period described on page 203.

First, step behind the girl's chair. Pull it away from the table just enough so that the girl can enter easily. As she lowers herself into the chair, gently slide the chair toward her. Be careful not to bump the edge of the seat into her legs. After she is seated, the girl may rise again slightly to allow you to slide her chair a little closer to the table. When dining at a restaurant with a girl, the headwaiter may help seat the girl. If not, you should perform this courtesy before you seat yourself.

Don't hog the floor space!

No matter how long your legs may be, don't usurp someone else's leg space. Remember, there are normally twice as many feet and legs under the table as there are heads above! Keep your feet pulled back just in front of your chair so that your legs are at right angles to your thighs. Do not let your knees spread out and bump the person next to you.

Think about the other guests!

Try to make your dinner partners feel comfortable by conversing pleasantly with them. If a serving dish is in front of you, the hostess may ask you to start passing it. Normally food is passed to the right. If the serving dish is heavy or awkward to handle, hold it for the guest next to you as he serves himself. When a serving dish is passed to you, remember to pass it on to the next person. Don't lay it down in front of you once you've taken your share! Use your eyes. Look around. Think of others. Make sure they are not sitting there with their mashed potatoes becoming cold because you've "docked" the gravy boat squarely in front of you and are carrying on a continuous conversation which they cannot interrupt. Remain attentive to the needs of others. Offer to pass the jelly or the rolls, etc. without waiting to be asked.

Don't reach in front of your neighbor to "long-arm" a roll! Wait for the "green light." Then simply say, "Would you please pass the rolls?" And remember to say "thank you!"

Observe common decencies.

Never dip your own used utensil into any common serving dish. When served from a common dish, take the food nearest you whether or not it is the most desirable piece. Do not take "seconds" until you have finished "firsts."

Don't "elbow" others.

Granted, it's easier to cut your meat when you have plenty of operating room. But most dinner tables do not allow un- limited elbow space for each guest. And even if the space were available, you would present an abnormal and unsightly picture cutting your meat with your elbows flying high, spread out like chicken wings. Train yourself to tuck your elbows close to your sides, making sure you keep your knife and fork in a horizontal position as close to the plate as possible — never vertical — while performing the cutting operation.

This skill may also be practiced during the Demonstration and Practice Period.

DON'T EAT LIKE "MR. REPULSIVE"

Read the items listed beneath this heading in the Student's Training Manual. Make comments as follows:

Watch your posture at the table.

Do you have to sit stiff and straight? No, you should be relaxed — but not slouched. Don't tip backward in your chair or drape your arm over the back of your chair. Don't hunch over your food plate, and don't circle your arm around it as though to protect your food from others. When not in use, your hands should be in your lap — not lying on the table.

And don't eat as though you had no arm muscle. Lift your food to your mouth. Don't duck your head down for each bite as though you were bobbing for apples at a Hallowe'en party!

Don't talk with food in your mouth.

If someone should ask you a question immediately after you've taken a bite, stall for a moment by taking a sip of water. This will help you to swallow the bite. Then proceed with your answer. Because conversation is a pleasant part of dining, it's a good idea to take smaller bites of food. In this way you'll be able to add to the conversation without having to stall for time or talk with food in your mouth.

Keep your mouth closed when chewing. Clean off the spoon or fork completely before you draw it out of your mouth.

Don't use your fingers as "food pushers."

If you cannot capture peas with your fork, use a crust of bread for a "pusher." Or take your knife in your left hand and use it as a barricade, so that you can retrieve the wandering food with your fork.

Special precautions are required when drinking.

Never take more than one or two sips of liquid at a time. Then you'll never become so out of breath that you have to exhale loudly when finished drinking. To avoid leaving a food smear around the rim of your glass, wipe your lips with your napkin before you take a drink. To avoid leaving beverage "rings" around your mouth, wipe your lips with your napkin after taking a drink, also. If you stir your hot beverage with a spoon to cool it, be sure to remove the spoon before you drink.

What to do when you have to blow your nose.

If you find that you must give your nose a slight blow at the table, do it as quietly and quickly as possible, turning your head away from the table. (Be sure you have a clean hand-kerchief in your pocket!) For a major nose-blowing project, excuse yourself and go to the bathroom (or some place where the other guests will not see or hear you.)

Do not discuss revolting subjects

Avoid talking about any subject that might bring unpleasant pictures into the minds of the guests or that might cause tension or arguments.

Avoid gruesome accident descriptions or discussions of operations or bodily injuries. Don't discuss topics that are related
to unpleasant odors — such as garbage, dead animals, sewer
drains, bad breath, or body perspiration.

Make no reference to bodily functions, sickness, upset
stomachs, nausea, etc.

Avoid discussing crimes of violence or disasters.

Why? Because unpleasant subjects not only spoil appetites,
but also hinder the operation of the digestive system, whereas
pleasant subjects are an aid to proper digestion and relaxed
enjoyment of the meal.

DO YOU KNOW WHAT THE WELL-MANNERED FELLOW DOES?

(Page 76, Student's Training Manual)

*Read the questions one at a time along with the multiple choice
answers. Give your students a few seconds to check their answers. Then
call for volunteers to share their ideas. Have your students correct the
answers in their manuals so that these pages will serve as a future guide
to proper etiquette. Correct answers and additional comments follow:*

1. When does the well-mannered fellow start eating?

At a small dinner party (of 6 or fewer guests) — (b) After
everyone else has been served, and the hostess has begun.

At a large dinner party — (b) After 4 or 5 have been served,
or the hostess says, "Please go ahead, so the food won't get
cold!"

2. Does he ever place his elbows on the table?

(c) Never while he is eating, but perhaps while resting between courses or conversing at the end of the meal.

Note: Never place your elbows on the table when you're
holding a knife, fork or spoon in your hand. Never place your
upper arm on the table. While waiting for the dinner to begin,
lay your hands in your lap.

3. Where does he leave his napkin throughout the meal?

(a) On his lap.

Note: You may wedge a corner of your napkin into your belt if you feel it's necessary. This is better than having it slide to the floor to tangle with your feet. But don't tuck your napkin under your chin. Leave a large dinner-size napkin folded in half. Unfold a luncheon-size napkin completely. Open your napkin quietly — not with a big shake!

4. What does he do with his napkin when he leaves the table?

(c) He lays it in loose folds beside his plate.

Note: Do not lay your napkin on the table as long as you are seated at the table. Even though you are finished eating, keep your napkin on your lap until you leave the table. If you excuse yourself in the middle of the meal, lay it beside your plate until you return.

5. How does he pass a pitcher?

(a) He hands it to the next person with the handle turned toward that person.

6. What does he do if the hostess serves food he doesn't like?

(b) He keeps quiet about it and takes a small portion anyway.

Note: You never have to accept "seconds"!

7. How does he serve himself gravy from the gravy boat?

(c) He dips gravy with the gravy ladle.

Note: Never pour it!

8. When butter or jelly is passed, where does he place it?

(a) He puts it on his plate, then transfers it to his bread or roll.

9. When "finger foods" such as olives, cookies, or sandwiches are passed around the table, what does he do with them?

(a) He places them on his plate, then transfers them to his mouth.

Note: Food is **never** transferred from a common serving dish into your mouth as long as you have a plate in front of you. If you are being served appetizers in the living room prior to the meal and have no plate, then of course you may transfer the food from the tray to your mouth.

10. How does he know which silver to use?

(b) He starts at the outside and works in toward his plate as the meal progresses.

Note: This is the **general** rule. Exceptions, however, can occur.

(c) When in doubt, he follows the lead of his hostess.

11. What does he do with his knife and fork after using them?

(c) He lays them flat across the side of his plate.

(Call attention to illustrations "What to do with your knife and fork after using them," top of page 78, Student's Training Manual.)

Note: When soup is served in a cup, lay the spoon on the dish under it when you are finished. When soup is served in a soup plate, however, leave the spoon in the soup plate. A dessert spoon is left on the dessert plate. When dessert is served in a sherbet glass or bowl, lay the spoon on the dish under it. (Spoons should always be left with the bowl of the spoon up.)

12. What does he do with his silver when passing his plate for "seconds"?

(b) He lays his knife and fork side by side across his plate.

Note: Place them carefully across the top portion of your plate so there's no danger of their falling off en route. Once you have used a utensil, allow **no portion of it** (not even the handle) to touch the table again.

13. How much meat does he cut at one time?

(b) He cuts one bite at a time as he eats it.

14. What implements could he use on the following items?

(Make certain that the students realize that more than one implement may be checked for an item.)

Fresh grapes, cherries, plums — **Fingers.**

Pickles, radishes, olives — **Fingers.**

French-fried potatoes — **(4) Dinner fork (at a dinner), or Fingers when eating informally.**

Corn on the cob — **Fingers.**

Pudding, custard, ice cream — **(6) Teaspoon.**

Fried chicken — **(1) Dinner knife, (4) Dinner fork and Fingers.**

Note: When the chicken is fried crisp and the occasion is an informal one — such as a picnic, you may eat it with your fingers. Bite the meat away from the bone as you hold it between your fingers. When served chicken at a **formal** dinner, cut away the meat from the bone using your knife and fork. When served chicken at an **informal** dinner, cut as much chicken as possible from the bone. Then holding the bone in one hand, you may eat the remaining meat from the bone as neatly as possible.

Sandwiches — (1) Dinner knife, (4) Dinner fork, or Fingers.

Note: Any hot sandwich covered with a sauce requires knife and fork. Some club sandwiches may also require a knife and fork, but may be eaten with the fingers if it can be done successfully. Open face sandwiches may be eaten with the fingers.

Moist cake — **(3) Salad or dessert fork.**

Celery or carrot sticks — **Fingers.**

Mashed potatoes and gravy — **(4) Dinner fork.**

Baked potato — **(1) Dinner knife, (4) Dinner fork.**

Note: Eat the inside of the potato with a fork, holding the tines up. If you want to eat the skin along with the inside of the potato, use your knife and fork to cut away a small portion at a time.

Nuts and mints — **Fingers.**

Cantaloupe section — **(6) Teaspoon.**

Watermelon section — **Either (3) Salad or dessert fork, or (4) Dinner fork.**

Note: Use your fork to pick away the seeds, then cut the melon into bite size pieces using the side of your fork.

Seafood cocktail — **(7) Oyster fork.**

Pie with ice cream — **(3) Salad or dessert fork.**

Note: Ice cream eaten alone is eaten with a spoon. When ala mode, it is eaten with a fork to avoid having to change implements repeatedly.

To butter corn on the cob — **(1) Dinner knife.**

Note: Butter and salt only a few rows at a time holding the cob carefully. Take one bite at a time. Do not munch from one end to the other like a "mowing machine."

To butter baked potato — **(4) Dinner fork.**

To butter bread or roll — **(2) Butter spreader (if available), or (1) Dinner knife.**

15. How does he butter his bread?

(a) He breaks off and butters a portion at a time. (e) He holds it on his plate (or slightly above).

Note: The same rule applies to rolls and muffins.

16. How does he eat his soup?

(b) He dips his soup spoon away from his body.
(c) He sips from the side of the spoon.
(f) He holds large crackers in his hand, but puts small oyster crackers in his soup, a few at a time.

17. How does he remove seeds, pits, gristle from his mouth?

(a) He takes unchewable food items out of his mouth in the same way they went in — with his fingers, fork, or spoon.

Note: If an unchewable item went in with your fingers, it comes out with your fingers. Therefore olive pits, grape seeds, fresh fruit pits, etc. are removed with the fingers.

If it went in with a spoon, it comes out on a spoon. Therefore stewed fruit pits, etc. are removed with a spoon.

If it went in with a fork, it comes out on a fork. Therefore meat gristle, etc. is removed with a fork. One exception: Though fish goes into your mouth with a fork, the bones may be removed with your fingers.

18. How does he handle problems or accidents at the table?

(a) In a prolonged siege of coughing or choking, he leaves the table.

Note: When personal problems occur at the table, try to call as little attention to yourself as possible.

(d) He leaves dropped silver on the floor until the end of the meal, and asks for a replacement if needed.

Note: An exception to this rule would be if the silver were covered with greasy or sticky food which could damage the rug.

(e) If he spills food and it's causing no harm, he goes on as though nothing had happened.

Note: If a spill might cause a stain, quickly scrape the food from the tablecloth with a clean knife. If you should knock over your water goblet, try to catch the water quickly with your napkin.

(g) If he splatters food on someone else, he apologizes and immediately offers his napkin.

19. If the hostess lingers at the table following the meal, what does he do?

(b) He stays at the table until she rises and says, "Shall we go into the living room?"

(c) If he has a pressing problem, he simply asks to be excused without making explanation.

DEMONSTRATION AND PRACTICE PERIOD (Optional)

Is there someone who can assist you with this lesson by acting as a "hostess"? Ask the "hostess" to set a table, if possible, using silver, napkins, water glasses, etc. This may be used as a "demonstration and practice table." Have the hostess identify and display the various pieces of utensils most commonly used, as well as their location beside the dinner plate.

Allow a few students at a time (depending upon the size of your class) to practice the following techniques as they are demonstrated:

1. WAITING FOR THE HOSTESS TO TELL THE GUESTS WHERE TO SIT.

2. SITTING DOWN AFTER THE HOSTESS IS SEATED.

3. HELPING SEAT THE "GIRL" AT THE RIGHT. (If girls are available, you may use them for this demonstration. If not, have your students practice this technique by taking turns assuming the role of the girl.) Call their attention to the illustration at the top of page 78.

4. UNFOLDING THE NAPKIN AND PLACING IT ON THE LAP. Note: You may ask the hostess to bring an example of a large dinner-size napkin and a luncheon-size napkin. Show the proper way to unfold each. Remind the students that napkins are to be opened quietly — not with a loud shake!

5. ASSUMING PROPER TABLE POSTURE, FEET IN FRONT OF CHAIR, ONE HAND IN LAP WHILE EATING WITH FORK, ETC.

6. EATING SOUP FROM A SOUP DISH. Make sure the students dip the spoon away from their body, sipping from the side of the spoon, leaving the spoon in the soup dish when finished. If soup is served as a first course, the soup spoon will be placed on the outside at the right.

7. CUTTING FOOD WITH KNIFE AND FORK. First, demonstrate the wrong way to perform this operation. (This will impress your students with the awkward and displeasing impression it gives.) To demonstrate the wrong way, hold your knife and fork almost vertically on your plate with wrists held high over the plate and elbows lifted high (almost equal with shoulders).

To demonstrate the correct way, keep the knife and fork as close to a horizontal position as possible with your hands held low to the plate and your elbows close at your sides.

When a student practices this technique, make certain that other "guests" are seated on either side of him so that he can judge whether or not his elbows are protruding into their area.

8. PASSING PLATE FOR "SECONDS." Show the students the proper way to place their utensils on their plates before passing for "seconds." See illustration at top of page 78 in Student's Training Manual.

9. DRINKING. Practice using napkin before and after drinking liquids.

10. PASSING OBJECTS. Pass a pitcher or gravy boat making sure each student turns the handle toward the next "guest," etc.

HOW TO MAKE INTRODUCTIONS
(Page 78, Student's Training Manual.)

Hve your students read the pointers listed here, then make comments as follows:

What is an introduction?

An introduction is simply a way of telling two or more people each other's names in order to acquaint them with each other.

When introducing two persons, the younger is introduced to the older, the man is introduced to the woman, and the boy is introduced to the girl. This is to show special honor and respect to those of greater age, as well as to women and girls. A distinguished celebrity or one of high rank or eminence is also honored in this way. The one of lower rank or eminence is introduced to the one of higher rank.

A good rule to follow is this:

Turn first toward the one being given this "first place of honor" and speak the name of this "first place" person **first**. For example: "**Grandmother**, this is my classmate, Jack Jones. Jack

— my grandmother, Mrs. Dugan." Or, **"Reverend Brown,** this is my cousin, Bobby Jackson." (Notice that you do not simply say, "This is my cousin, Bobby." An introduction is incomplete without last names.

Refer your students to the illustrations at the bottom of page 78. In each of the illustrations, the boy in the middle position is making an introduction. Those being introduced are identified in the captions below. Have your students write appropriate introductions.

Suggested answers are as follows:

• "Father, this is my friend, Mary Green."

Rule: Introduce the younger person to the older person. (A girl under 18 years of age is regarded as a young person. If Mary were older than 18, the introduction would be that of a man to a woman: "Mary, this is my father. Dad — Mary Green."

• "Mrs. Green, this is my mother."

Rule: Introduce your mother or father to your friend's mother or father. (It is not necessary to give your mother's last name if her name is the same as yours.)

• "Mary, this is Bob Brown. Bob — Mary Green."

Rule: Introduce a boy to a girl. (Notice that Bob must be informed of Mary's last name.)

• "Mrs. Moore, this is Mary Green."

Rule: Introduce a younger person to an older person.

• "Dr. Holcomb, this is my father."

Rule: Introduce your mother or father to your school principal, coach or teacher.

WHAT'S WRONG IN THESE PICTURES?
(Page 79, Student's Training Manual)

Have your students examine carefully the four illustrations at the top of page 79 to determine what the boy is doing wrong in each instance. Ask your students to write their ideas in the spaces provided in their Training Manuals. Have them share their ideas. Correct answers follow:

Illustration No. 1

As a mark of respect a boy should rise to his feet when an older person enters the room for the first time. He should offer his seat when other seating is not available or is not as comfortable. A boy should also stand when a guest is leaving his home.

Illustration No. 2

When dining in a restaurant with a girl, the boy asks the girl what she would like. He then places their order with the waitress, giving the girl's order first if it differs from his.

Illustration No. 3

A boy holds an umbrella for the girl and himself. A boy carries any bulky or heavy packages for the girl. A boy normally walks on the outer lane of the sidewalk (but is not required to switch back and forth for short distances). When walking with two girls, the boy should not walk between them. This would force him to twist his head **away** from one when talking to the other. When walking in an outside position, he can talk to both, looking in **one** direction.

Illustration No. 4

A boy helps a girl put on her coat. He holds it at the fold of the lapels, being careful not to hold it too high and thereby make it difficult for the girl to position her hands in the armholes. When seated in an auditorium, a boy helps a girl remove her coat and arranges it over the back of the seat for her.

DATING "DO'S" AND "TABOO'S"

Have your students mark the statements in their Student Training Manuals as either "Do" or "Taboo." Answers are as follows:

Do   — When asking for a date, telephone as early as possible.

Taboo — Wait till the last minute to phone.

Do — When you say "Hello", give your first and last name.

Taboo — Keep her guessing! Say, "Guess who!"

Taboo — Ask, "Are you busy Friday night?"

Do — First, tell her what you have in mind for Friday night.

Do — Give her the facts she needs concerning the date.

Taboo — Skip the details!

Do — Call for her at her front door.

Taboo — Sit in the car and honk!

Taboo — When invited in, say "No thanks, I'll just wait here!"

Do — Go inside, meet her parents, and visit briefly with them.

Taboo — When your date enters the room, stay seated.

Do — When your date enters the room, rise to your feet.

Do — At the end of the evening, return her to her door safely.

Taboo — Just reach across, open the car door, and let her out.

WHO GOES FIRST?

Have your students check whether a boy or girl goes first in the instances given in their Student Training Manuals. Correct answers are as follows:

1. (Girl) — A boy always allows a girl to get on a bus, train or subway first.

2. (Boy) — A boy steps off first, then turns to offer the girl his hand as she descends.

3. (Girl) — A boy allows a girl to go through an open doorway ahead of him.

4. (Boy) — Coming up to a closed door, the boy steps forward and pulls open the door for the girl, holding it while the girl passes through. If the door opens away from him and is very heavy, it may be necessary for him to step through the doorway first.

5. (Boy) — When there is no hostess or headwaiter, the boy leads the way to the table, and the girl follows him.

6. (Girl) — When following a hostess or headwaiter, the girl precedes the boy.

7. (Boy) — When walking down a darkened auditorium aisle with no usher present, the boy leads the way.

8. (Girl) — When following an usher down an auditorium aisle, the girl precedes the boy.

9. (Girl) — A boys stands aside and allows a girl to precede him when entering a row of seats.

10. (Girl) — A girl enters an automobile first after the boy has opened the car door for her. If he is driving, he shuts the door for her, then goes around the car to the driver's seat.

11. (Boy) — A boy gets out of an automobile first, then opens the door for the girl.

12. (Boy) — A boy goes down a narrow, steep stairway ahead of the girl. This is so that he can offer her his hand to help steady her. In any hazardous situation, the boy always precedes the girl.

WHY SHOULD CHRISTIANS PRACTICE GOOD MANNERS?
(Page 79, Student's Training Manual)

Have your students read aloud the 5 reasons given here, together with the accompanying scripture verses. Make additional comments as follows:

Why should the "Man in Demand" practice good manners?

The "Man in Demand" should practice good manners because rudeness and crudeness will hinder him as he seeks to serve God and man. Inconsiderate, unmannerly ways will cause doors of opportunity to be closed to him. Repulsive manners will keep others at arm's length. If he fails to practice courtesy, which is the exercise of good manners, he will not be able to make his influence count towards changing the world for God.

Courtesy enhances every other skill.

The manly skills that the "Man in Demand" has developed will count for little — if they are not enhanced by the crowning grace of courtesy. The apostle Paul told the Corinthian believers that without love, their most noteworthy talents and deeds would profit them nothing.

(Briefly review the 13th chapter of 1 Corinthians with your students.)

Courtesy is love in action.

In a very real sense, courtesy is akin to love. For courtesy is simply showing love by doing those things that **please,** and refraining from those things that **annoy.** With this in mind, let's consider for a moment how this 13th chapter of 1 Corinthians might be paraphrased to apply to the "Man in Demand" and the importance of courtesy in his life.

COURTESY AND THE "MAN IN DEMAND"

Though I speak with skill and cleverness — **and have not courtesy** — I am merely clogging the sound waves!

Though I hold my head high and step out straight and tall like a man — **and have not courtesy** — I'm getting nowhere!

Though I shave, comb and scrub, though I jog, walk and run, though I dress with neatness and finesse — **and do not practice courtesy** — I amount to little!

Though I discipline my body with one hundred push-ups daily — **and do not practice courtesy** — I'm just fooling myself. I'm not a success at all!

Courtesy is thoughtful and kind. It never embarrasses others or makes them appear awkward. It thinks of others first and self last. It doesn't hog the show, nor does it throw its weight around or walk on others' toes. Courtesy steps softly, speaks gently, showing honor and regard to all.

Though other feats a man performs may be empty puffs of wind, courtesy never fails. For courtesy is love in action, and love will last forever!

Prayer:

Father, we often forget to be thoughtful of others. We act before we think. And when we do think — we think about ourselves! Forgive us. And teach us to respect and honor all men, so that we may bring honor to the name of your Son, Jesus Christ. Amen.

Memory Question No. 13: How can we show concern for the feelings of others?

Answer: "Having compassion one of another, love as brethren . . . be courteous" (1 Peter 3:8).

MAN IN DEMAND
COMPLETION PROGRAM

To climax the Man in Demand Training Course, invite the parents of your students to a completion program. (Or you may prefer to have a Father-Son Banquet.) A completion program will not only give the students an opportunity to display what they have learned but will also provide an occasion for familiarizing members of your community with your organization.

The following program ideas are given as suggestions only. Don't stifle your own creative abilities. Knowing your own students and their individual talents, you may come up with some new and exciting ideas for this program.

PROGRAM INTRODUCTION (by the teacher).

Welcome to the Completion Program for our "Man in Demand" Training Course! Perhaps you've been wondering what the fellows have been learning during our training sessions. This is your opportunity to find out!

First of all, you may have wondered why this course is called the "Man in Demand" Training Course. There's a good reason. It's because **real** men are **in demand** these days! People are **demanding** leaders they can trust — men of stature and integrity! They're seeking disciplined, wide-awake young men who possess manly strengths and sterling qualities. This is the kind of man God is seeking, too! And this is the kind of man this course is designed to produce!

At the outset, each fellow faced an urgent call. Listen as _____ reads this call for you, as it appears in each boy's Training Manual. *Have a student read from page 4 of the Training Manual. "Wanted! Today's Youth to Become God's Man of Tomorrow." Continue as follows:*

"Do you dare to become the Man in Demand?" This was a serious question. Before it could be answered, it was necessary for each fellow to come to grips with the matter of his own personal identity. **"Who am I? Why am I here?"** For logically there was no reason for him to be concerned with the kind of man he might become unless he knew that his life had meaning and purpose! One of the things that each fellow discovered as he looked into this question was that his life was important to God because he, himself, was a totally **unique** person!

This is how it was expressed in the boy's Training Manuals. Listen as _____ reads it for us.

Have a student read from page 12 of the Student's Training Manual. "I Am Unique in This World." Continue as follows:

"What shall I do with this person I call 'me'?" Each fellow had to face up to this pressing question. A decision had to be made before proceeding further. Our Training Manuals showed us exactly what kind of challenge lay before each one of the fellows. _____ will read this for us from his Training Manual.

Have a student read from page 13 of the Student's Training Manual, "My Decision." Continue as follows:

And so _____ weeks ago these fellows placed themselves in training to become the "Man in Demand." What did this training involve? We'll let the students themselves tell you!

Have your students describe to their parents the various principles of manliness presented during each lesson. If your class is large, you may wish to choose two boys to tell about each lesson, one describing the practical physical and social helps which were given, and the other telling about the moral and spiritual qualities which are necessary to total manliness.

Though the boys should present this in their own words, describing their own impressions, they'll appreciate suggestions from you. They may want you to review with them some of the instruction included in your Teacher's Book. If time is limited, you may want the students to present only a few select lessons as a sample of the kind of training received.

SUGGESTIONS FOR YOUR STUDENTS

Select from the following those which appeal most to your group:

1. Read the poem, "The Man in Demand," page 5, Student's Training Manual. Tell what it meant to you personally. Or describe the steps in Joe's Futile Search for Identity, page 7.

2. Tell about the fingerprinting operation and the students' attempts to identify one another through their fingerprints.

3. Perform the Conversational Skit and tell what you learned from it.

4. Act out several of the "posture cartoons," pages 21 − 24, Student's Training Manual, and tell what they taught you about the power of a boy's posture.

5. Demonstrate good posture and bad posture. Demonstrate the Pencil Test and the Plumb Line Test.

6. Give a light-hearted demonstration of "Four Sure Ways to Make a Bad Impression When Seated," or "Three Sure Ways to Harass Your Hostess," page 26, Student's Training Manual.

7. Describe how a boy's facial appearance is like a computer "Print-Out" of his "Heart In-Put" as shown on pages 34 and 35 of the Training Manual.

8. Describe the two "Merry-Go-Rounds" and how a fellow gets on or off them, page 45, Student's Training Manual. Tell about Successful Sam, Lazy Larry and Mac the Muncher, or perform the skit.

9. Demonstrate a fellow's "Daily Half-Dozen," page 50, Student's Training Manual.

10. Act out the "clothing cartoons" on page 55, Student's Training Manual. Tell what they taught you.

11. Present some of the thoughts given on page 57, Student's Training Manual, "Does Belonging to Christ Make a Difference in the Way a Young Man Dresses?"

12. Describe the problems faced by Petrified Pete, Fidgety-Freddie, Howard-the-Coward, Dudley the Dud, Over-Spruced Bruce, and Over-Awed Claude (page 67, Student's Training Manual) and tell what advice they needed to hear.

CONCLUSION

Musical Number: Have your group sing the song, "Is It You?" (See the inside back cover of Training Manual.) Or ask several talented vocalists and instrumentalists in your group to present this.

Concluding Remarks: Ask a pastor to give a few remarks on the subject, "Fulfilling Your Role as the Man in Demand" following the thoughts expressed on page 80 of the Training Manual. Or you, as teacher, may want to express these thoughts to your class as a final word of benediction to them, adding your own personal expressions.

VERSION 1 - RICK'S PART

As the skit opens, "Rick" and "Marie" are seated side by side before the class, holding paper plates and napkins in their laps. Using a fork, they go through the motions of eating as they speak.

<u>Rick:</u> Hi, Marie! This strawberry shortcake sure tastes good, doesn't it! It's my favorite dessert.

* Marie: It is?

<u>Rick:</u> Yeah . . . I never get tired of eating strawberries!

* Marie: *(Without enthusiasm)*, Oh . . .

<u>Rick:</u> I've been picking strawberries all week, and I still like to eat 'em!

* Marie: *(Bored)*, Well . . .

<u>Rick:</u> Yeah, and if I pick fast enough, I make pretty good money! I'm saving for a ten-speed bike!

* Marie: Hmmm . . .

<u>Rick:</u> Yeah, and I'm gonna travel to the coast next year with Bill.

* Marie: *(Looking aside as though trying to find a way of escape)*, Well . . .

<u>Rick:</u> Yeah! Bill's already bought his bike! It's really great!

* Marie: Ho . . . hum . . . *(Yawns loudly, closes eyes, droops head as though to fall asleep.)*

End of Skit — Version One — *(Players remain seated.)*

VERSION 1 - MARIE'S PART

As the skit opens, "Rick" and "Marie" are seated side by side before the class, holding paper plates and napkins in their laps. Using a fork, they go through the motions of eating as they speak.

* Rick: Hi, Marie! This strawberry shortcake sure tastes good, doesn't it! It's my favorite dessert.

<u>Marie:</u> It is?

* Rick: Yeah . . . I never get tired of eating strawberries!

<u>Marie:</u> *(Without enthusiasm)*, Oh . . .

* Rick: I've been picking strawberries all week, and I still like to eat 'em!

<u>Marie:</u> *(Bored)*, Well . . .

* Rick: Yeah, and if I pick fast enough, I make pretty good money! I'm saving for a ten-speed bike!

<u>Marie:</u> Hmmm . . .

* Rick: Yeah, and I'm gonna travel to the coast next year with Bill.

<u>Marie:</u> *(Looking aside as though trying to find a way of escape)*, Well . . .

* Rick: Yeah! Bill's already bought his bike! It's really great!

<u>Marie:</u> Ho . . . hum . . . *(Yawns loudly, closes eyes, droops head as though to fall asleep.)*

End of Skit — Version One — *(Players remain seated.)*

Rick: Hi, Marie! This strawberry shortcake sure tastes good, doesn't it! It's my favorite dessert. What's yours?

* Marie: *(Brightly)*, Oh . . . I'd say it's the wild blackberry pie Mom bakes at our summer cabin!

Rick: Oh? Do you have a cabin? Where is it?

* Marie: In the Blue Mountains! They're beautiful! Ever been there?

Rick: Sure! I go fishing there with my Dad. And when we're not fishing, we're hiking. What do you like to do in the mountains, Marie?

* Marie: Oh, I like to swim . . . and hike . . . and study the birds. Have you ever noticed how many blue jays there are?

Rick: Sure have! They're so noisy you can't miss 'em! And have you noticed the wild pigeons?

* Marie: Yes! And the woodpeckers, too! You know, Rick . . . I've counted as many as 14 different species of birds near our cabin, but I don't know all their names.

Rick: Say, Marie . . . I've got a Bird Book! Maybe you'd like to take it with you next time you go! Can I bring it over sometime?

* Marie: *(Brightly)*, Sure thing! That'll be great! Thanks a lot, Rick!

End of Skit — Version Two

VERSION 2 - MARIE'S PART

* Rick: Hi, Marie! This strawberry shortcake sure tastes good, doesn't it! It's my favorite dessert. What's yours?

Marie: *(Brightly)*, Oh . . . I'd say it's the wild blackberry pie Mom bakes at our summer cabin!

* Rick: Oh? Do you have a cabin? Where is it?

Marie: In the Blue Mountains! They're beautiful! Ever been there?

* Rick: Sure! I go fishing there with my Dad. And when we're not fishing, we're hiking. What do you like to do in the mountains, Marie?

Marie: Oh, I like to swim . . . and hike . . . and study the birds. Have you ever noticed how many blue jays there are?

* Rick: Sure have! They're so noisy you can't miss 'em! And have you noticed the wild pigeons?

Marie: Yes! And the woodpeckers, too! You know, Rick . . . I've counted as many as 14 different species of birds near our cabin, but I don't know all their names.

* Rick: Say, Marie . . . I've got a Bird Book! Maybe you'd like to take it with you next time you go! Can I bring it over sometime?

Marie: *(Brightly)*, Sure thing! That'll be great! Thanks a lot, Rick!

End of Skit — Version Two

Sam is at home making a telephone call. *(Sam makes motions as though dialing.)*

*Mac: *(Swallowing hard and licking his lips as he picks up the phone.)* (Gulp!) Hello!

Sam: Hi, Mac! This is Sam! Did I get you from something?

*Mac: Naw ... I was just finishing a jelly doughnut left over from breakfast. What's on your mind? *(Mack picks up potato chip box and smiles with anticipation as he peers into it.)*

Sam: Oh, nothing special! Didn't get to see you at school yesterday. How'd it go for you?

*Mac: *(Grabbing a handful of potato chips out of the box and chewing on them noisily.)* Oh ... (chomp, chomp) ... pretty boring, I'd say ... (chomp, chomp) that is, until I stopped at the Ice Cream Shoppe on the way home (chomp, chomp). That hot fudge sundae really hit the spot! (chomp, chomp.)

Sam: What'd you say? I'm having a hard time hearing you. There's some loud crackling in my ear! We must have a bad connection!

*Mac: *(Still munching.)* That's funny ... (chomp, chomp) I can hear you just fine! Let's see now, what have I been doing? Well, I went to Boy's Club last night, but it was sure dull! That is, until they brought out the cupcake and hot chocolate. I woke up fast then! Professor Perkins should have seen me! He complains about me being lethargic and dull in his English class!

Sam: Yea, the Prof is pretty demanding! His tests are sticklers too! That reminds me ... have you studied for the test he's giving Monday?

*Mac: Yeah ... I hit the books when I got home from the Boy's Club meeting. But studying late makes me famished! Had to raid the refrigerator to survive! Boy, Mom makes the best apple pie!

Sam: Say, Mac ... they're holding Junior Varsity try-outs Monday. Are you going to show up?

*Mac: Naw! No use, Sam! The coach has it in for me! Says I'm too slow! He's sure unreasonable! Can I help it if I'm just naturally heavy? How about you, Sam? Will you try out?

Sam: Sure thing!

*Mac: Well, with your physique, they'll grab you fast! Some guys are born lucky! *(Heaves a big sigh.)* Not me though! *(Droops his shoulders.)* Man, I'm low on energy this morning! I need an early lunch today. I'd better call you back after I've eaten. But wait ... I see my lazy brother's finally crawled out of bed! Wanna talk to him?

Sam: Sure ... put him on! *Larry walks into room, yawning and stretching.*

*Mac: *(Handing phone to Lazy Larry.)* Here, Larry ... it's Sam!

*Larry: *(Drowzily, still standing.)* Hi, Sam ... how're things?

Sam: Really great, Larry! But where were you yesterday? Missed you in gymn class!

*Larry: Oh, I got excused! Told Mr. Harris I was dizzy! Well ... I did feel sort of tired ... and it was a relief to get out of that hurdle-leaping! Who wants to play like a leap-frog anyway!

Sam: Did you get to the game after school?

*Larry: Naw ... I borrowed a bus pass and rode downtown to the main library to check out a book I've been wanting to read. My old man thought I should've walked! But he forgets how tired a guy gets sittin' in a stuffy old school building all day! *(Pauses, and looks around.)* Just a minute Sam. I want to take a seat here! *(Sinks into the chair, heaving a big sigh as though exhausted.)* Guess I got out of bed too early this morning. I'm one of those guys that requires lots of rest!

Sam: Sure, Larry! Are you O.K. now?

*Larry: Yeah . . . I think so. Now, where were we? Oh, yeah . . . the library. Well, I got a science fiction book, and spent the rest of the day in bed reading! It was really neat! But what's new with you, Sam?

Sam: Well . . . for one thing, I'm going swimming this afternoon! How about coming along?

*Larry: *(Shaking his head firmly.)* No, siree! Not me! Today's my only day to rest! And besides, I want to finish this book to see if the space man captures the Mars monster or not.

Sam: But I'll see you at the Youth Skate tonight, won't I?

*Larry: Naw . . . not much reason for me to go. The girls don't skate with me anyway! They all cluster around you, Sam! Wonder what makes them so unfriendly! *(Stretching.)* Ho . . . hum! Just talking about skating makes me tired all over! Maybe if I get comfortable here, I'll feel better. *(Sprawling out on floor, and propping his feet up on a chair.)* Yeah . . . this is more like it! *(Sighs pleasantly.)* Now, Sam, I want to hear how your day went yesterday. I'll just rest here while you talk.

Sam: Well, Larry, I really had a red letter day! Awoke feeling great . . . got off to my usual good start . . . and the whole day just fell in place — like that!

*Larry: Hold on here a minute . . . what do yah mean —your "usual good start?" You got a secret formula or something?

Sam: Oh, no . . . not anything special . . . really . . . I just kick back the covers every morning . . . jump out of bed and do some deep-breathing exercises before I get dressed. Then I read my Bible, eat breakfast and go off to school feeling like a winner!

*Larry: Ugh! Sounds awful to me! Too much exertion so early in the morning! But speaking of winners . . . who won the game yesterday after school?

Sam: We did! Trimmed Stanley High 81 to 60! Somehow I managed to make 14 baskets! Everyone gathered around to talk afterward, and I missed my bus home. Didn't mind the walk though.

*Larry: Did you stop at the Ice Cream Shoppe?

Sam: Nope! I'm in training! And besides, I wanted to be able to enjoy a good square meal when I got home! So I just ate the apple I'd saved from lunch. Ran into Betty though, and we had a real good time talking all the way home!

*Larry: Are you taking her to the Youth Skate tonight?

Sam: No, but she asked if I'd be there . . . and she looked real happy when I said I would. She said she'd be seeing me! Come to think of it . . . I sure did have a good day!

*Larry: Glad someone did! *(Yawn . . .)* Guess I'd better hang up now. This phone is getting . . . awfully . . . heavy . . . *(Drops head on his chest, letting receiver drop.)*

Sam: *(Listening for a moment.)* Larry? Larry?

*Larry: *(Making loud snoring noise.)* Zzzz . . . Zzzz . . . Zzzz . . .

Sam: *(Shaking head and hanging up phone.)* Hmm . . . It's easy to see that Mac the Muncher and Lazy Larry are both trapped on the wrong merry-go-round! They should read page 45 in the Training Manual!

END OF SKIT

Mack the Muncher enters from side hall, walks slowly toward the table, chewing obviously as he picks up the receiver. (To free his hands, Mac lays his lines on the table in front of him.)

Mac: *(Swallowing hard and licking his lips as he picks up the phone.)* (Gulp!) Hello!

*Sam: Hi, Mac! This is Sam! Did I get you from something?

Mac: Naw ... I was just finishing a jelly doughnut left over from breakfast. What's on your mind? *(Mack picks up potato chip box and smiles with anticipation as he peers into it.)*

*Sam: Oh, nothing special! Didn't get to see you at school yesterday. How'd it go for you?

Mac: *(Grabbing a handful of potato chips out of the box and chewing on them noisily.)* Oh ... (chomp, chomp) ... pretty boring, I'd say ... (chomp, chomp) that is, until I stopped at the Ice Cream Shoppe on the way home (chomp, chomp). That hot fudge sundae really hit the spot! (chomp, chomp.)

*Sam: What'd you say? I'm having a hard time hearing you. There's some loud crackling in my ear! We must have a bad connection!

Mac: *(Still munching.)* That's funny ... (chomp, chomp) I can hear you just fine! Let's see now, what have I been doing? Well, I went to Boy's Club last night, but it was sure dull! That is, until they brought out the

---

LARRY'S PART

Larry: *(Drowzily, still standing.)* Hi, Sam ... how're things?

*Sam: Really great, Larry! But where were you yesterday? Missed you in gymn class!

Larry: Oh, I got excused! Told Mr. Harris I was dizzy! Well ... I did feel sort of tired ... and it was a relief to get out of that hurdle-leaping! Who wants to play like a leap-frog anyway!

*Sam: Did you get to the game after school?

Larry: Naw ... I borrowed a bus pass and rode downtown to the main library to check out a book I've been wanting to read. My old man thought I should've walked! But he forgets how tired a guy gets sittin' in a stuffy old school building all day! *(Pauses, and looks around.)* Just a minute Sam. I want to take a seat here! *(Sinks into the chair, heaving a big sigh as though exhausted.)* Guess I got out of bed too early this morning. I'm one of those guys that requires lots of rest!

*Sam: Sure, Larry! Are you O.K. now?

Larry: Yeah . . . I think so. Now, where were we? Oh, yeah . . . the library. Well, I got a science fiction book, and spent the rest of the day in bed reading! It was really neat! But what's new with you, Sam?

*Sam: Well ... for one thing, I'm going swimming this afternoon! How about coming along?

Larry: *(Shaking his head firmly.)* No, siree! Not me! Today's my only day to rest! And besides, I want to finish this book to see if the space man captures the Mars monster or not.

*Sam: But I'll see you at the Youth Skate tonight, won't I?

Larry: Naw ... not much reason for me to go. The girls don't skate with me anyway! They all cluster around you, Sam! Wonder what makes them so unfriendly! *(Stretching.)* Ho . . . hum! Just talking about skating makes me tired all over! Maybe if I get comfortable here, I'll feel better. *(Sprawling out on floor, and propping his feet up on a chair.)* Yeah ... this is more like it! *(Sighs pleasantly.)* Now, Sam, I want to hear how your day went yesterday. I'll just rest here while you talk.

cupcake and hot chocolate. I woke up fast then! Professor Perkins should have seen me! He complains about me being lethargic and dull in his English class!

* Sam: Yea, the Prof is pretty demanding! His tests are sticklers too! That reminds me ... have you studied for the test he's giving Monday?

Mac: Yeah ... I hit the books when I got home from the Boy's Club meeting. But studying late makes me famished! Had to raid the refrigerator to survive! Boy, Mom makes the best apple pie!

* Sam: Say, Mac ... they're holding Junior Varsity try-outs Monday. Are you going to show up?

Mac: Naw! No use, Sam! The coach has it in for me! Says I'm too slow! He's sure unreasonable! Can I help it if I'm just naturally heavy? How about you, Sam? Will you try out?

* Sam: Sure thing!

Mac: Well, with your physique, they'll grab you fast! Some guys are born lucky! *(Heaves a big sigh.)* Not me though! *(Droops his shoulders.)* Man, I'm low on energy this morning! I need an early lunch today. I'd better call you back after I've eaten. But wait ... I see my lazy brother's finally crawled out of bed! Wanna talk to him?

* Sam: Sure ... put him on! *Larry walks into room, yawning and stretching.*

Mac: *(Handing phone to Lazy Larry.)* Here, Larry ... it's Sam!

---

* Sam: Well, Larry, I really had a red letter day! Awoke feeling great ... got off to my usual good start ... and the whole day just fell in place — like that!

Larry: Hold on here a minute ... what do yah mean —your "usual good start?" You got a secret formula or something?

* Sam: Oh, no ... not anything special ... really ... I just kick back the covers every morning ... jump out of bed and do some deep-breathing exercises before I get dressed. Then I read my Bible, eat breakfast and go off to school feeling like a winner!

Larry: Ugh! Sounds awful to me! Too much exertion so early in the morning! But speaking of winners ... who won the game yesterday after school?

* Sam: We did! Trimmed Stanley High 81 to 60! Somehow I managed to make 14 baskets! Everyone gathered around to talk afterward, and I missed my bus home. Didn't mind the walk though.

Larry: Did you stop at the Ice Cream Shoppe?

* Sam: Nope! I'm in training! And besides, I wanted to be able to enjoy a good square meal when I got home! So I just ate the apple I'd saved from lunch. Ran into Betty though, and we had a real good time talking all the way home!

Larry: Are you taking her to the Youth Skate tonight?

* Sam: No, but she asked if I'd be there ... and she looked real happy when I said I would. She said she'd be seeing me! Come to think of it ... I sure did have a good day!

Larry: Glad someone did! *(Yawn . . .)* Guess I'd better hang up now. This phone is getting ... awfully ... heavy ... *(Drops head on his chest, letting receiver drop.)*

* Sam: *(Listening for a moment.)* Larry? Larry?

Larry: *(Making loud snoring noise.)* Zzzz ... Zzzz ... Zzzz ...

* Sam: *(Shaking head and hanging up phone.)* Hmm ... It's easy to see that Mac the Muncher and Lazy Larry are both trapped on the wrong merry-go-round! They should read page 45 in the Training Manual!

END OF SKIT

(1) MR. INFERIOR'S PART

I'm Mr. Inferior. Everyone else seems better than me. *(Hang head.)* I don't measure up to the other kids. When I'm around a big shot, he overwhelms me and I feel like a "nobody"! The big shot seems so important, I'm afraid to open my mouth. Wish I could feel self-confident like the other guys, but I guess they're just better than me! I'll probably be an awkward mess all my life! *(Shake head slowly.)* But what can I expect when I'm so inferior? *(Clasp hands in front and hang head.)*

(2) MR. INADEQUATE'S PART

I'm Mr. Inadequate. When I'm up against a new situation, I get flustered and embarrassed! *(Swing body in an embarrassed manner.)* I don't know how to act! *(Shuffle feet.)* I wonder if I'm saying the right thing and if I'm dressed right. *(Look down at clothes.)* I feel like I'm "on the spot," and I get so nervous I can't enjoy myself! And I can't enjoy anyone else either! Sometimes I wish I'd just stayed home because I feel so inadequate." *(Shrug shoulders. Lift hands in helpless, bewildered manner.)*

(3) MR. FEARFUL'S PART

I'm Mr. Fearful. What do I fear? Everything! I fear I'll look foolish or make a bad impression. *(Appear timid and frightened. Chew on fingernails.)* I'm afraid others are laughing at me behind my back. *(Twist around as though looking behind.)* I'm afraid I'll be a failure and others will reject me. And when I get scared, I can't do anything right! I stiffen up ... *(pull up rigidly)* ... I stumble over furniture ... *(stumble over other foot)* ... I blush and st-st-st-st-stam-m-mer ... and I don't know what to do with my hands! *(Shove hands in pockets. Pull them out again. Try to hide them.)* I imagine that every eye is upon me. It ruins my fun. I'm so full of fears, I'm just plain miserable! *(Assume trembling, fearful pose similar to that in Training Manual.)*

(4) MR. SELF-CONCERNED'S PART

I'm Mr. Self-Concerned. I can't get my mind off myself! Sure, I'm aware the other guy is there ... but my main concern is "What does he think of me?" *(Point to self.)* Do I wonder if anyone else is having a good time? *(Motion toward others.)* No! It's me I'm worrying about! *(Point to self again.)* Do I wonder how others feel? No! I'm too occupied with my own feelings to be concerned about theirs! I'm constantly on guard to make sure I don't "lose face"! And this keeps my eyes constantly on me! Me! Me! *(Point repeatedly toward self.)*

(5) MR. GUILTY'S PART

I'm Mr. Guilty. When I'm running with the wrong gang and doing things I shouldn't do ... my conscience hurts! *(Hunch shoulders and look around uneasily.)* I've found out that when I'm doing wrong, I can't feel right. And with these bad things gnawing at my conscience, I feel ill at ease — even when I'm with the right gang! I find myself thinking, "Boy, I hope they never find out!" *(Shield face with hand, as though to hide from others.)* Or, "Would they really like me if they knew?" Putting up a false front makes me so jittery, I can't act natural. *(Shake head sadly.)* It's hard to relax and be happy when you've got a guilty conscience.